CIM

PRACTICE & REVISION KIT

Advanced Certificate

The Marketing Customer Interface

BPP Publishing
September 2000

First edition 1999
Second edition September 2000

ISBN 0 7517 4909 5 (previous edition 0 7517 4924 9)

British Library Cataloguing-in-Publication Data
A catalogue record for this book
is available from the British Library

Published by

BPP Publishing Limited
Aldine House, Aldine Place
London W12 8AW

www.bpp.com

in association with
Nottingham Business School
Nottingham Trent University

Printed in Great Britain by W M Print
45 – 47 Frederick Street
Walsall
West Midlands, WS2 9NE

We are grateful to the Chartered Institute of Marketing for permission to reproduce past examination questions. The suggested solutions to past examination questions have been prepared by BPP Publishing Limited.

Author
Debbie Gilliland

Series editor
Paul Brittain, Senior Lecturer in Marketing and Retailing at Nottingham Business School, Nottingham Trent University

CONTENTS

BPP PUBLISHING

The headings indicate the main topics of questions, but questions often cover several different topics.

Tutorial questions, listed in italics, are followed by **guidance notes** on how to approach the question, thus easing the transition from study to examination practice.

A date alone (6/99, say) after the question title refers to a past examination question.

Questions marked by * are **key questions** which we think you should attempt to give yourself the best chance of passing the exam. Tick them off on this list as you complete them.

> **Note:** Questions worth 10 marks will only occur in the exam of the part of the 40 mark case study.

BPP PUBLISHING

ABOUT THIS KIT

You're taking your professional CIM exams in December 2000 and June 2001. You're under time pressure to get your exam revision done and you want to pass first time. Could you make better use of your time? Are you sure that your revision is really relevant to the exam you will be facing?

If you use this BPP Practice & Revision Kit you can be sure that the time you spend revising and practising questions is time well spent.

The BPP Practice & Revision Kit: The Marketing Customer Interface

The BPP Practice & Revision Kit, produced in association with Nottingham Trent University Business School, has been specifically written for the syllabus by an expert in marketing education, Debbie Gilliland.

- We give you a comprehensive question and answer checklist so you can see at a glance which are the key questions that we think you should attempt in order to pass the exam, what the mark and time allocations are and when they were set (where this is relevant)

- We offer vital guidance on revision, question practice and exam technique

- We show you the syllabus examinable in December 2000 and June 2001. We analyse the papers set so far, with summaries of the examiner's comments

- We give you a comprehensive question bank containing:

  ○ *Do You Know* checklists to jog your memory

  ○ *Tutorial questions* to warm you up

  ○ *Exam-standard questions*, including questions set up until December 1999 and the new syllabus specimen paper

  ○ *Full suggested answers* - with summaries of the examiner's comments

- A **Test Your Knowledge quiz** covering selected areas from the entire syllabus

- A **Test Paper** consisting of the June 2000 exam, again with full suggested answers, for you to attempt just before the real thing

- A **Topic Index** for ready reference

The Study Text: further help from BPP

The other vital part of BPP's study package is the Study Text. The Study Text features:

- Structured, methodical syllabus coverage

- Lots of case examples from real businesses throughout, to show you how the theory applies in real life

- Action programmes and quizzes so that you can test that you've mastered the theory

- A question and answer bank

- Key concepts and full index

There's an order form at the back of this Kit.

Help us to help you

Your feedback will help us improve our study package. Please complete and return the Review Form at the end of this Kit; you will be entered automatically in a Free Prize Draw.

BPP Publishing September 2000

To learn more about what BPP has to offer, visit our website: www.bpp.com

---

REVISION

This is a very important time as you approach the exam. You must remember three things.

> **Use time sensibly**
> **Set realistic goals**
> **Believe in yourself**

Use time sensibly

---

1   **How much study time do you have?** Remember that you must EAT, SLEEP, and of course, RELAX.

2   **How will you split that available time between each subject?** What are your weaker subjects? They need more time.

3   **What is your learning style?** AM/PM? Little and often/long sessions? Evenings/ weekends?

4   **Are you taking regular breaks?** Most people absorb more if they do not attempt to study for long uninterrupted periods of time. A five minute break every hour (to make coffee, watch the news headlines) can make all the difference.

5   **Do you have quality study time?** Unplug the phone. Let everybody know that you're studying and shouldn't be disturbed.

Set realistic goals

---

1   Have you set a **clearly defined objective** for each study period?

2   Is the objective **achievable?**

3   Will you **stick to your plan?** Will you make up for any **lost time?**

4   Are you **rewarding yourself** for your hard work?

5   Are you leading a **healthy lifestyle?**

Believe in yourself

Are you cultivating the right attitude of mind? There is absolutely no reason why you should not pass this exam if you adopt the correct approach.

•   **Be confident** - you've passed exams before, you can pass them again

•   **Be calm** - plenty of adrenaline but no panicking

•   **Be focused** - commit yourself to passing the exam

QUESTION PRACTICE

Do not simply open this Kit and, beginning with question 1, start attempting all of the questions. You first need to ask yourself three questions.

> **Am I ready to answer questions?**
> **Do I know which questions to do first?**
> **How should I use this Kit?**

Am I ready to answer questions?

1   Check that you are familiar with the material on the **Do you know?** page for a particular syllabus area.

2   If you are happy, you can go ahead and start answering questions. If not, go back to your BPP Study Text and revise first.

Do I know which questions to do first?

1   **Start with tutorial questions**. They warm you up for key and difficult areas of the syllabus. Try to produce at least a plan for these questions, using the guidance notes following the question to ensure your answer is structured so as to gain a good pass mark.

2   Don't worry about the time it takes to answer these questions. Concentrate on producing good answers.

How should I use this Kit?

1   Once you are confident with the Do you know? checklists and the tutorial questions, you should try as many as possible of the exam-standard questions; at the very least you should attempt the **key questions,** which are highlighted in the **question and answer checklist/index** at the front of the Kit.

2   Try to **produce full answers under timed conditions**; you are practising exam technique as much as knowledge recall here. Don't look at the answer, your BPP Study Text or your notes for any help at all.

3   **Mark your answers to the non-tutorial questions as if you were the examiner**. Only give yourself marks for what you have written, not for what you meant to put down, or would have put down if you had had more time. If you did badly, try another question.

4   Read the **Tutorial notes** in the answers very carefully and take note of the advice given and any **comments by the examiner**.

5   When you have practised the whole syllabus, go back to the areas you had problems with and **practise further questions**.

6   When you feel you have completed your revision of the entire syllabus to your satisfaction, answer the **test your knowledge** quiz on pages 141 to 144. This covers selected areas from the entire syllabus and answering it unseen is a good test of how well you can recall your knowledge of diverse subjects quickly.

7   Finally, when you think you really understand the entire subject, **attempt the test paper** at the end of the Kit. Sit the paper under strict exam conditions, so that you gain experience of selecting and sequencing your questions, and managing your time, as well as of writing answers.

EXAM TECHNIQUE

Passing professional examinations is half about having the knowledge, and half about doing yourself full justice in the examination. You must have the right approach to two things.

> ## The day of the exam
> ## Your time in the exam hall

The day of the exam

1   Set at least one alarm (or get an alarm call) for a morning exam.

2   Have something to eat but beware of eating too much; you may feel sleepy if your system is digesting a large meal.

3   Allow plenty of time to get to the exam hall; have your route worked out in advance and listen to news bulletins to check for potential travel problems.

4   Don't forget pens, pencils, rulers, erasers.

5   Put new batteries into your calculator and take a spare set (or a spare calculator).

6   Avoid discussion about the exam with other candidates outside the exam hall.

Your time in the exam hall

1   **Read the instructions (the 'rubric') on the front of the exam paper carefully**

Check that the exam format hasn't changed. It is surprising how often examiners' reports remark on the number of students who attempt too few - or too many - questions, or who attempt the wrong number of questions from different parts of the paper. Make sure that you are planning to answer the right number of questions.

2   **Select questions carefully**

Read through the paper once, then quickly jot down key points against each question in a second read through. Select those questions where you could latch on to 'what the question is about' - but remember to check carefully that you have got the right end of the stick before putting pen to paper.

3   **Plan your attack carefully**

Consider the order in which you are going to tackle questions. It is a good idea to start with your best question to boost your morale and get some easy marks 'in the bag'.

4   **Check the time allocation for each question**

Each mark carries with it a time allocation of 1.6 minutes (including time for selecting and reading questions). A 20 mark question therefore should be completed in 32 minutes. When time is up, you must go on to the next question or part. Going even one minute over the time allowed brings you a lot closer to failure.

5   **Read the question carefully and plan your answer**

Read through the question again very carefully when you come to answer it. Plan your answer to ensure that you keep to the point. Two minutes of planning plus eight minutes of writing is virtually certain to earn you more marks than ten minutes of writing.

6   **Produce relevant answers**

Particularly with written answers, make sure you answer the question set, and not the question you would have preferred to have been set.

7   **Gain the easy marks**

Include the obvious if it answers the question and don't try to produce the perfect answer.

Don't get bogged down in small parts of questions. If you find a part of a question difficult, get on with the rest of the question. If you are having problems with something, the chances are that everyone else is too.

8   **Produce an answer in the correct format**

The examiner will state in the requirements the format in which the question should be answered, for example in a report or memorandum.

9   **Follow the examiner's instructions**

You will annoy the examiner if you ignore him or her. The examiner will state whether he or she wishes you to 'discuss', 'comment', 'evaluate' or 'recommend'.

10   **Present a tidy paper**

Students are penalised for poor presentation and so you should make sure that you write legibly, label diagrams clearly and lay out your work neatly. Markers of scripts each have hundreds of papers to mark; a badly written scrawl is unlikely to receive the same attention as a neat and well laid out paper.

11   **Stay until the end of the exam**

Use any spare time checking and rechecking your script.

12   **Don't worry if you feel you have performed badly in the exam**

It is more than likely that the other candidates will have found the exam difficult too. Don't forget that there is a competitive element in these exams. As soon as you get up to leave the exam hall, *forget* that exam and think about the next - or, if it is the last one, celebrate!

13   **Don't discuss an exam with other candidates**

This is particularly the case if you still have other exams to sit. Even if you have finished, you should put it out of your mind until the day of the results. Forget about exams and relax!

APPROACHING MINI-CASES

What is a mini-case?

The mini-case in the examination is a 500-800 word long description of an organisation at a moment in time. You first see it in the examination room and so you have 64 minutes to read, understand, analyse and answer the mini-case.

The mini-case (Part A of the paper) carries 40% of the available marks in the examination.

As mini-cases are fundamental to your exam success, you should be absolutely clear about what mini-cases are, the CIM's purpose in using them, and what the examiner seeks; then, in context, you must consider how best they should be tackled.

The purpose of the mini-case

The examiner requires students to demonstrate not only their knowledge of the fundamentals of marketing, but also their ability to use that knowledge in a commercially credible way in the context of a 'real' business scenario.

The examiner's requirements

The examiner is the 'consumer' of your examination script. You should remember first and foremost that a paper is needed which makes his or her life easy. That means that the script should be well laid out, with plenty of white space and neat readable writing. All the basic rules of examination technique discussed earlier must be applied, but because communication skills are fundamental to the marketer, the ability to communicate clearly is particularly important.

An approach to mini-cases

Mini-cases are easy once you have mastered the basic techniques. The key to success lies in adopting a logical sequence of steps which, with practice, you will master. You must enter the exam room with the process as second nature, so you can concentrate your attention on the marketing issues which face you.

Students who are at first apprehensive when faced with a mini-case often come to find them much more stimulating and rewarding than traditional examination questions. There is the added security of knowing that there is no single correct answer to a case study.

Suggested mini-case method

You have about 64 minutes in total.

Stage		*Minutes*
1	Read the mini-case and questions set on it very quickly.	2
2	Read the questions and case again, but carefully. Make brief notes of significant material. Determine key issues in relation to the questions etc.	5
3	Put the case on one side and turn to your notes. What do they contain? A clear picture of the situation? Go back if necessary and concentrate on getting a grip on the scenario outlined.	4
4	Prepare an answer structure plan for question (a) following exactly the structure suggested in the question, highlighting your decisions supported by case data and theory if appropriate. Follow the process outlined for question (b), etc.	3
5	Prepare a timeplan for each part of the question, according to the marks allocated.	1
6	Write your answer.	44
7	Read through and correct errors, improve presentation.	5
		64

(xii)

A good answer will be a document on which a competent manager can take action.

Notes

(a) It is not seriously suggested that you can allocate your time quite so rigorously! The purpose of showing detailed timings is to demonstrate the need to move with purpose and control through each stage of the process.

(b) Take time to get the facts into your short term memory. Making decisions is easier once the facts are in your head.

(c) Establish a clear plan and you will find that writing the answers is straightforward.

(d) Some candidates will be writing answers within five minutes. The better candidates will ignore them and concentrate on planning. This is not easy to do, but management of your examination technique is the key to your personal success.

(e) Presentation is crucial. Your answer should be written as a final draft that would go to typing. If the typist could understand every word and replicate the layout, then the examiner will be delighted and it will be marked highly.

Handling an unseen mini-case in the examination

The following extract is taken from a Chartered Institute of Marketing's Tutor's/Student Guide to the treatment of mini-cases.

Tutor's/Student Guide to the treatment of mini-cases

'It needs to be stated unequivocally that the type of extremely short case (popularly called the mini-case) set in the examinations for Certificate and Diploma subjects cannot be treated in exactly the same way as a long case study issued in advance. If it could there would be little point of going to all the trouble of writing an in-depth case study.

'Far too many students adopt a maxi-case approach using a detailed marketing audit outline which is largely inappropriate to a case consisting only of two or three paragraphs. Others use the SWOT analysis and simply re-write the case under the four headings of strengths, weaknesses, opportunities and threats.

'Some students even go so far as to totally ignore the specific questions set and present a standard maxi-case analysis outline including environmental reviews through to contingency plans.

'The "mini-case" is not really a case at all, it is merely an outline of a given situation, a scenario. Its purpose is to test whether examinees can apply their knowledge of marketing theory and techniques to the company or organisation and the operating environment described in the scenario. For example answers advocating retail audits as part of the marketing information system for a small industrial goods manufacturer demonstrate a lack of practical awareness. Such answers confirm that the examinee has learned a given MIS outline by rote and simply regurgitated this in complete disregard of the scenario. Such an approach would be disastrous in the real world and examinees adopting this approach cannot be passed, ie gain the confidence of the Institute as professional marketing practitioners. The correct approach to the scenario is a mental review of the area covered by the question and the *selection* by the examinee of those particular parts of knowledge or techniques which apply to the case. This implies a rejection of those parts of the student's knowledge which clearly do not apply to the scenario.

'All scenarios are based upon real world companies and situations and are written with a fuller knowledge of how that organisation actually operates in its planning environments. Often the organisation described in the scenario will not be a giant fast moving consumer goods manufacturing and marketing company since this would facilitate mindless

BPP PUBLISHING

regurgitation of textbook outlines and be counter to the intention of this section of the examination.

'More often the scenarios will involve innovative small or medium sized firms which comprise the vast majority of UK companies which lack the resources often assumed by the textbook approach. These firms do have to market within these constraints however and are just as much concerned with marketing communications, marketing planning and control and indeed (proportionately) in international marketing, particularly the Common Market, as are larger enterprises.

'However, as marketing applications develop and expand and as changes take root, the Institute (through its examiners) will wish to test students' knowledge and awareness of these changes and their implication with regard to marketing practice. For example in the public sector increasing attention is being paid to the marketing of leisure services and the concept of "asset marketing" where the "product" is to a greater extent fixed and therefore the option of product as a variable in the marketing mix is somewhat more constrained.

'Tutors and students are referred to Examiners' Reports which repeatedly complain of inappropriateness of answer detail which demonstrates a real lack of *practical* marketing grasp and confirms that a leaned by rote textbook regurgitation is being used. Examples would include:

- The recommendation of national TV advertising for a small industrial company with a local market

- The overnight installation of a marketing department comprising Marketing Director, Marketing Manager, Advertising Manager, Distribution Manager, Sales Manager, etc into what has been described as a very small company

- The inclusion of packaging, branded packs, on-pack offers, etc, in the marketing mix recommendations for a service

'It has to be borne in mind that the award of the Diploma is in a very real sense the granting of a licence to practice marketing and certainly an endorsement of the candidate's practical as well as theoretical grasps of marketing. In these circumstances such treatments of the mini-case as described above cannot be passed and give rise to some concern that perhaps the teaching/learning approach to mini-cases has not been sufficiently differentiated from that recommended for maxi-cases.

'Tutors/distance-learning students are recommended to work on previously set mini-cases and questions and review results against published specimen answers. They are also advised to use course-members' companies/organisations as examples in the constraints/limitations of marketing techniques and how they might need to be modified.

'Students are also advised to answer the specified questions set and if for example a question was on objectives, then undue reference to market analysis and strategies would be treated as extraneous.'

THE EXAM PAPER

Format of the exam

The exam is based on a mini-case describing a business situation.

		Number of marks
Part A:	compulsory question relating to the mini-case	40
Part B:	Three questions from a choice of six	60
		100

Analysis of past papers

Question number in this Kit

June 2000
Part A (Compulsory case study: 40 marks)

1 A chemical company experiencing departmental conflict and lacking a customer focus
   (a) The causes of conflict and possible remedies
   (b) Promoting customer-facing attitudes and behaviour
   (c) Improving communication with customers
   (d) Soliciting customer feedback

Part B (three from six: 20 marks each)

2 Demographics and segmentation – older people
3 Impact of electronic commerce
4 Customer service and competitive advantage
5 Marketing research plan
6 Avoiding losing touch with customers
7 Segmentation

> This paper forms the Test Paper at the end of this Kit.

December 1999

Part A (Compulsory case study: 40 marks)

1 A production orientated printing company   81
   (a) Customer feedback – obtaining, analysing and acting on
   (b) Relationship marketing
   (c) Encouraging a customer focus
   (d) Creating a competitive advantage

Part B (three from six: 20 marks each)

2	Customer value and profitability	5
3	Attitude formation and change	64
4	The effect of 'issues' on customer behaviour	79
5	The changing human involvement in providing service	16
6	Customer satisfaction and customer delight	78
7	Creating an organisational climate characterised by innovation and speed	17

The exam paper

SYLLABUS

Aims and objectives

- To provide students with an understanding of the application of fundamental marketing principles and concepts within a variety of organisations

- To develop an appreciation of the importance of a broad range of relevant information to support an organisation's marketing activities

- To emphasise the importance of developing appropriate internal and external business relationships on a local, regional and global basis

- To develop the application of key skills including: IT, numeracy, problem solving and communications across a range of marketing activities

- To equip students with an awareness of how marketing tools, activities and opportunities are used in a marketing and project-planning context

- To provide opportunities to integrate and apply the CIM Certificate modules Marketing Fundamentals, Customer Communications and Marketing Environment

Learning outcomes

Students will be able to:

- Recognise the importance of collecting relevant data, and the variety of information sources, both primary and secondary

- Formulate recommendations based on information from multiple sources

- Recognise key relationships inside and outside the organisation and demonstrate an awareness of methods of developing relationships

- Apply planning techniques to a range of marketing tasks and activities

- Evaluate and select media and promotional activities in line with the organisation's objectives and status

- Analyse current usage of the extended marketing mix

- Calculate and justify budgets for marketing mix decisions

- Evaluate marketing results against financial and other criteria

BPP PUBLISHING

Indicative content and weighting

1 Overview, concepts and background   *(study weighting 10%)*

1.1 *Terminology and definitions*

- Identifying 'customer', 'user', 'consumer' and 'payer': interpretations of customer focus in organisations
- Assumptions, stereotypes and myths about the marketing/customer interface and customer dynamics

1.2 *The emergence of customer power in the new competitive climate*

- Driving forces and organisational responses
- Significance for the marketing/customer interface

1.3 *Customer-focused marketing in specific economic sectors*

- Customer orientation within major profit-seeking and competitive arenas and within not-for-profit organisations

2 Managing the marketing/customer interface   *(study weighting 30%)*

2.1 *The strategic dimension: vision and leadership*

- Corporate strategy, culture and structure; the role of top-down leadership, vision, empowerment and related processes
- Systems for simulating customer-focused behaviour within and across organisations
- Customer focus, customer relationships, retention, and customer service as key ingredients in the drive for sustainable competitive advantage
- The functional/organisational aspects of customer focus: accountability in the fields of customer focus and customer service
- The strategic rationale for outsourcing: benefits, risks, applications, goal-setting and monitoring
- Customer-related measures as part of the corporate scorecard

2.2 *The managerial dimension: mobilising performances*

- Key factors in maximising the corporate benefits from the organisation/ customer interface: information technology and people management
- Motivational issues and job design for front-line customer-facing roles
- The impact and implications of electronic commerce in the field of customer relationships - the richness/reach dilemma

2.3 *Creating positive relationships with customers*

- The features, benefits and costs of relationship marketing
- Methods of communicating with customers
- Customer/supplier partnership and agreements

2.4 *Innovation and the culture of continuous improvement*

- Sources of customer-focused innovation; barriers to implementation and how to overcome them
- The role of information-gathering and analysis in generating customer-focused product/service innovation

3 Customer dynamics
(study weighting 25%)

3.1 *The holistic perspective of customer behaviour*

- Modelling customer dynamics: rationale, objectives, applications, limitations
- Individuals, groups and organisations as customers
- Innovation and conservatism in customer behaviour: why new products/ services succeed or fail
- Customer expectations and perceptions: dissatisfaction, satisfaction and delight

3.2 *Classifying customers for competitive advantage*

- Customer segmentation: rationale, objectives; features of effective customer segments
- Segmentation systems for individual consumers, customer groups and organisations
- New approaches to classifying customers

3.3 *The individual as customer*

- Attitudes and behaviour: relevance to the marketing/customer interface
- Factors influencing the individual's behaviour as a customer
- Personality profiling for individual customers

3.4 *The group as customer*

- Power, influence and authority within the primary group: targeting the decision-making unit (DMU)
- Secondary groups: their significance for customer behaviour and implications for national, international and global marketing

3.5 *The organisation as customer*

- Special features of business-to-business transactions and related customer dynamics
- The organisational DMU: characteristics, roles, decision processes and marketing implications

4 Investigating customer dynamics
(study weighting 20%)

4.1 *Basic principles*

- Systematic techniques for investigating customer dynamics
- The creation of meaningful populations (based on market segments)

4.2 *Quantitative methodologies for investigating customer dynamics*

- Questionnaires, surveys, interviews and other primary methods of data/ information collection

4.3 *Qualitative methodologies for investigating customer dynamics*

- Projective techniques: features, benefits, risks and applications
- Focus groups: features, benefits, risks and applications

4.4 *Secondary information sources*

- Sources of secondary data: government statistics, market research agencies, the media etc

BPP PUBLISHING

5 Customer dynamics and the future *(study weighting 15%)*

5.1 *Trends in customer behaviour and expectations*

- Enhancement of customer expectations and organisational service standards and performance delivery
- Increasing opportunities for customer complaints and legal enhancements to consumer power
- Customer concerns about ecological, environmental and ethical issues
- Emergent customer attitudes and their impact on (re)purchasing behaviour
- Future patterns for segmentation: customised products and services, demographic and social trends etc

5.2 *Market trends with customer-facing implications*

- The global marketplace and global products and services
- Customer service as a sustainable competitive advantage
- The decline of manufacturing and the emergence of new service-sector industries

5.3 *The marketing implications of e-commerce*

- Emergent business models in the age of e-commerce
- Trends in e-commerce with special reference to business to consumer, business to business, utilities and public sector applications
- Strategic, organisational and managerial issues associated with the achievement of competitive advantage in an e-commerce market place
- Internet marketing and the significance of e-commerce for supplier/customer relationships

Question bank

DO YOU KNOW? – THE MARKETING CUSTOMER INTERFACE - OVERVIEW

- *Check that you know the following basic points before you attempt any questions. If in doubt, you should go back to your BPP Study Text and revise first*

- Because the decision-making unit comprises a number of individuals, and the decision-making process is often a lengthy and complex one, there is an important distinction to be made between customers - who buy the product/service - and users, who make use of its provision.

- Customers may be within an organisation as well as external to it.

- The Decision Making Unit is the group of people who come together to influence, positively or negatively, a purchase decision. They usually comprise gatekeepers, initiators, influencers, deciders, buyers, users and financiers. An individual may occupy, concurrently or consecutively, more than one role in the unit. Reaching the key figures in the DMU is a crucial role of the marketer.

- Central to the principle of marketing-led organisations is the process of getting to know our customers. They need first to be identified before they are understood.

- The marketing concept has three elements:
  - ○ customer orientation
  - ○ co-ordination of market-led activities
  - ○ generally, a profit orientation

- Until relatively recently many organisations were able to regard their customers with indifference. Command-and-control cultures thrived; there was no expectation that employees could make a difference.

- Increasing competition has meant that organisations have to change.

- Customers are much less tolerant and are willing to complain if they have a grievance.

- When customers walk into a shop, or phone the customer complaints line, they want the company's employees to own the problem. They do not want to be passed around the houses; they do not want to be told about the organisation's difficulties ('we're very short-staffed at the moment' or 'the computer's down' or 'she's at lunch'); even less do they want to hear the employee adding some complaints of his own about the way he is treated.

- Customer care is 'a fundamental approach to the standards of service quality. It covers every aspect of a company's operations, from the design of a product or service to how it is packaged, delivered and serviced.'

- Relationship marketing is one development that reflects growing customer power.

- Many public sector organisations have benefited from implementing a competitive philosophy.

- Electronic commerce is having a profound effect on the retail sector.

- Domestic lifestyles have changed, as have attitudes to work and leisure. This has affected the retailing environment and purchasing habits.

- IT has also had an effect on the manufacturing sector but it remains true that many business-to-business customers for complex products value the face-to-face approach.

> **Note.** Questions worth **10 marks will only occur in the exam as part of the 40 mark case study**. The 10 mark questions within this Question bank will help you approach those questions confidently.

1 TUTORIAL QUESTION: CUSTOMERS AND USERS   *16 mins*

Some organisations distinguish between 'customers' (defined as people who buy the product or service on offer) and 'users' (people who use it but without paying anything directly themselves).

Write a report in which you discuss the merits of this distinction, and its marketing implications, as if you were an advisor to the marketing department of either a toy manufacturer or a large retailer of motor cars.   **(10 marks)**

2 KNOWING AND UNDERSTANDING THE CUSTOMER   *16 mins*

Even if Drucker is right in claiming that the aim of marketing is to make selling superfluous, what are the practical problems associated with 'knowing and understanding the customer so well that the product or service ... sells itself?"

(10 marks)

3 CONSUMER POWER   *16 mins*

What are the reasons for the increasing awareness of consumer rights and greater interest in the consumer movement?   **(10 marks)**

4 CUSTOMER ORIENTATION   *16 mins*

Discuss what is meant by the term customer orientation. What are its advantages?

(10 marks)

5 CUSTOMER VALUE AND PROFITABILITY (12/99)   *32 mins*

According to Hugh Davidson (*Even More Offensive Marketing*, Penguin Books, 1997), every employee's job should be specified and evaluated against only two parameters: 'contribution to consistently superior customer value' and 'contribution to above-average profits'. How far do you agree? What would be the problems of implementing Davidson's idea with regard to any **one** of the following occupational roles?

(a) A shift manager in a factory
(b) A research and development scientist
(c) A human resources officer
(d) A management accountant

(20 marks)

DO YOU KNOW? – MANAGING THE MARKETING CUSTOMER INTERFACE

- *Check that you know the following basic points before you attempt any questions. If in doubt, you should go back to your BPP Study Text and revise first.*

- Structure has an impact on the culture of the organisation.

- Recent trends in marketing organisation include team-based working and the setting up of customer service departments.

- The societal marketing concept believes that the key task of the organisation is to determine the needs and wants of target markets. There is also increasing concern with ethical issues.

- Reichheld's Service Profit Cycle demonstrates the linkages between external service performance and internal strategy.

- Embedding a customer focused culture requires top management commitment. The senior examiner reinforces this with his model 'The 12 Pillars of Performance'.

- The value chain devised by Michael Porter highlights the marketing and sales function as an activity which can add value for the customer and be a key source of competitive advantage.

- The general change within organisational culture has generated a movement towards shedding or hiving off activities and giving them over to the control of independent managers. This is the process known as outsourcing.

- The balanced scorecard emphasises the need to provide information addressing all relevant areas of performance.

- A major impact of new technology is that firms are becoming increasingly aware of the competitive advantage that may be achieved. Information systems can affect the way the firm approaches customer service and can provide advantages over competitor approaches.

- Information can be viewed as a marketing asset. Database marketing allows vast amounts of customer data to be stored.

- A database is a coherent structure for the storage and use of data. Benefits of such systems might include:
    - increased sales and/or market share
    - increased customer retention
    - better use of resources
    - better decision-making

- E-commerce can reduce expensive sales and distribution workforces, and offers new marketing opportunities.

- To get a bird's-eye view of an organisation's operations is the purpose of the value chain model of corporate activities, developed by Michael Porter. The needs of the customer are affected by all the activities in the value chain.

- Leadership and people management have an important role to play in creating and maintaining a positive corporate culture, which will lead to success in such areas as customer focus and service.

- This chapter has also examined teamworking, recruitment and selection, development and training, rewards and incentives, and motivational issues.

- Nowadays, everyone in the organisation has to be measured against the extent to which they add value by making a contribution to the attainment of the corporate goals and vision.

- Customer service involves dealing with each complaint as it happens, and trying to pre-empt future complaints.

- Employees working in customer service areas should have their jobs designed so that they have some autonomy over the decisions to be made and responses and level of service to be given to customers.

- Recessionary pressures have encouraged processes such as delayering (cutting out levels of mainly middle-management) and downsizing, leading to 'flatter hierarchies', with more delegation and more decentralisation of authority.

- Increasingly popular in organisations - not always connected to the requirement for improved customer service - are competency frameworks which list the standard of behaviour required in any given job. Accountability profiles focus on results and outcomes.

- Internal marketing is a recognition that people who work together stand in exactly the same relationship to each other as do customers and suppliers.

- Customer profitability is the 'total sales revenue generated from a customer or customer group, less all the costs that are incurred in servicing that customer or customer group.' Businesses need to identify which of their customers generate the most profit.

- Activity based costing often confirms that some products and customers are profitable, but are subsidising those which make a loss.

- Long term relationships with customers are generally more profitable than one-off transactions.

- Loyalty can be defined as 'voluntary repurchasing and referral'.

- Marketers are increasingly classifying customers according to their level of commitment to brands, using terminology such as 'entrenched', 'average', 'shallow' or 'convertible'.

- The argument continues to rage about whether it is still legitimate to segment customers into large groups unified against only one dimension or whether segmentation is now dead and has been superseded by the ultimate segment of one: the individual customer.

- Relationship marketing changes the focus away from getting customers (which is still seen as vital) towards keeping customers. This change in emphasis is the most fundamental distinction.

- Customers can be regarded as assets because they can bring future benefits in the form of repeat business.

- Recently there has been a backlash against relationship marketing especially as applied to the consumer sector. Not all customers want a relationship and resent the potential intrusion.

- Customer care is fundamental to a marketing orientation.

- Customer feedback is an essential piece of management information and is a cheap source of market research.

- The Institute of Direct Marketing in the UK define direct marketing as 'The planned recording, analysis and tracking of customer behaviour to develop relational marketing strategies'. Direct marketing creates and develops a direct relationship between the customer and the company on an individual basis.

- E-commerce is an avenue for generating a close relationship between customer and supplier. But many companies engaging in e-commerce fail to capitalise on it.

- Innovation is making something new or doing something in a different way. It may be a new product, but it also covers new ways of satisfying customers, new ways of carrying out routine activities, new linkages in the value chain, new approaches to work and organisation structure. Innovation provides the organisation with a distinctive competence and can help to maintain competitive advantage.

- The term new product development encompasses a wide range of different types of activity ranging form the development of completely new products and technologies to repackaging of existing ones.

- The ideas driving innovation can come from anywhere in the organisation. The learning organisation encourages such knowledge generation.

- Benchmarking compares business operations with what is known to be best practice in other companies or industries.

- Corporate think-tanks and brainstorming sessions can also generate new ideas.

- There are various organisational barriers to innovation, including old structures, resistance to change and centralised control. Bureaucracy can stand in the way of innovation.

- Marketing research can assist in developing innovative ideas, by testing customer reactions.

6   TUTORIAL QUESTION: RELATIONSHIP MARKETING   *16 mins*

Discuss the marriage analogy and the relationship between organisations and their suppliers.   **(10 marks)**

7   BRAND EQUITY   *16 mins*

What is the concept of brand equity? What characteristics should a brand possess to acquire high brand equity?   **(10 marks)**

8   TRUST AND COMMITMENT   *16 mins*

Define the concepts of trust and commitment. What role do they play in relationship-based buying?   **(10 marks)**

9   STAFF MOTIVATION   *16 mins*

There is ongoing debate about the extent to which compensation, especially pay, is an employee motivator. One view, mostly associated with Herzberg, is that earnings do not cause motivation but do cause dissatisfaction if not adequately provided. How far do you agree with this view?   **(10 marks)**

10   VALUE FOR CUSTOMERS   *16 mins*

What is meant by effectiveness and efficiency in terms of creating value for customers? Why might both be important to marketers trying to deliver superior customer value?

(10 marks)

11   CUSTOMER SERVICE ENVIRONMENT   *16 mins*

The effect of music on shoppers is one example of how physical surroundings can influence buying. Identify five other means through which the physical surroundings can influence buying.   **(10 marks)**

12   THE SERVICE ENVIRONMENT   *16 mins*

Identify the key aspects of the service environment with reference to an example and discuss the impact they have on consumer behaviour.   **(10 marks)**

13   TECHNOLOGY   *16 mins*

Technological advances have been identified as a major market context factor and have been shown to affect customer behaviour in several different ways. Discuss these with examples.   **(10 marks)**

14   CUSTOMER SERVICE IN MANUFACTURING (SPECIMEN PAPER)   *32 mins*

It has been widely argued that, in the future, manufacturing companies will find it virtually impossible to remain profitable through reliance on manufacturing alone. As a result, they will be forced, whether they like it or not, to achieve competitive superiority (if they can) in such arenas as customer service and relationship marketing.

Why might it be thought that profitability from manufacturing alone is so problematic? In what specific ways can manufacturing companies ensure their continued success through customer service and relationship marketing? Illustrate your answer with relevant examples. **(20 marks)**

15 CUSTOMER-CENTRIC ORGANISATION (SPECIMEN PAPER) *32 mins*

What does the term 'customer-centric' mean when applied to the structure of an organisation engaged in either financial services OR retailing? Having produced your answer, discuss the features of any organisation known to you which in your judgement is not customer-centric, and outline what changes would need to be introduced if the organisation in question were to seek to become genuinely customer-centric. **(20 marks)**

16 CHANGES IN THE DELIVERY OF CUSTOMER SERVICE (12/99) *32 mins*

In *Business@The Speed of Thought* (Penguin Books 1999), Bill Gates of Microsoft predicts that 'Customer service will become the primary value-added function in every business. Human involvement in service will shift from routine, low-value tasks to a high- value, personal consultancy on important issues, problems or desires for the customer'.

What are the possible grounds for this prediction? Assuming that Gates is correct, what are the consequences for the way organisations are designed? **(20 marks)**

17 ENCOURAGING INNOVATION (12/99) *32 mins*

For the purposes of this question you should visualise yourself as a Marketing Consultant with a corporate client who is concerned about their inability to create exciting new products and services. They are also concerned about their slowness in bringing new products and services to the market place, compared with the innovation and speed demonstrated by some of their competitors. Your client has one question:

'What do we have to do in order to create an organisational climate which is characterised by innovation and speed?'

Draft your reply, in the form of a discussion document, addressed to your client's Marketing Director. **(20 marks)**

DO YOU KNOW? – CUSTOMER DYNAMICS

- *Check that you know the following basic points before you attempt any questions. If in doubt, you should go back to your BPP Study Text and revise first.*

- Consumer behaviour models are popular because, in the words of Keith Williams, 'it has ... been found that it is possible to simplify consumer behaviour into its principal components and that, in practice, a relatively small number of variables account for the vast bulk of consumer behaviour'.

- In the broadest sense customers fall into three 'types': individuals, groups and organisations.

- The rate and extent of diffusion of an innovation depend on:
  - the characteristics of the innovation/new product
  - the channels of communication used
  - the social system within which communication takes place
  - the stages of the adoption process reached by members of the social system

- Adopter categories have been identified as:
  - innovators
  - early adopters
  - early majority
  - late majority
  - laggards

- It is of crucial importance to the marketer of an innovation to know who the innovators/early triers are, and how they can be reached and influenced.

- The customer who is merely 'satisfied' is between 7 and 10 times more likely to move to another supplier than a customer who is 'very satisfied'. It is the 'very satisfied' customer who is genuinely loyal and will repurchase.

- The delighters are the features or characteristics which surprise customers positively.

- Segmentation groups customers according to identifiable characteristics relevant to their purchase behaviour. For a market to be usefully segmentable, it must be measurable, accessible and substantial.

- Demographics is the process by which a population is analysed according to the relevant characteristics it demonstrates, such as gender, age, occupation etc. Geo-demographics, combines these factors with geographical location.

- Status (power and authority) and the awareness of it allow marketers to position a product.

- Psychographics builds up a psychological profile of consumers in general, or of consumers of a particular product. Also known as lifestyle analysis, psychographics help to segment markets at the same time as suggesting concrete ways to appeal to particular segments.

- Family life-cycle analysis classifies families so as to give a composite picture of the family in terms of commonly-used demographic factors. There are various models of the FLC; Schiffman and Kanuk's has five stages.

  - Bachelorhood
  - Honeymooners
  - Parenthood ('full next')
  - Post-parenthood ('empty nest')
  - Dissolution

- There have been criticisms of the FLC in recent years.

  - It is modelled on patterns in industrialised western nations.
  - There are now important potential variations from the model.

- Because of the increasingly global nature of marketing, cross-cultural psychographics is of increasing interest to marketers, by which the different mind-sets of people from different cultures are analysed.

- Organisational markets are also open to segmentation.

- Individuals are important in all buying decisions, either for themselves or on behalf of an organisation. Marketers need to understand their motives, psychology and influences, and how these combine to form a motivation mix.

- A consumer's self-image may lead him to choose brands which support him and help him towards his expected self-concept.

- An attitude is a relatively consistent, learned predisposition to behave in a certain way in response to a given object.

- Attribution theory states that attitudes are formed by people's interpretations of their own behaviour and experiences.

- Consistency theories state that individuals seek cognitive consistency, experiencing tension if this is not achieved.

- Marketers often seek to change attitudes. Factors affecting attitude change are existing attitudes, source factors (who is telling us), message features, the communication channel, receiver attributes and product characteristics.

  The individual is influenced by his or her personal environment.

- Socialisation is the process by which knowledge of society and its rules is acquired, to enable participation in that society. The family is the earliest contact through which socialisation is achieved.

- Groups can serve as a benchmark for behavioural norms and specific attitudes.

- Reference groups influence buying decisions.

- Motivation can be understood by reference to needs, wants and goals.

- Be aware of motivation theories:
  - Maslow's hierarchy of needs
  - Alderfer's existence, relatedness and growth
  - McClelland's three motivating needs
  - Vroom's expectancy theory

  It is important to examine these in a marketing context.

- Trait factor theories and self concept theories can also assist the marketer.

- Marketers need to understand a buyer's motives, psychology and influences, and how these combine to form a motivation mix.

- The decision making unit (DMU) that operates most often is within a family context, with different family members adopting different consumption and hence DMU roles.

- Organisational decision-making is based on the same DMU model but is generally more rational yet inert. The interaction of DMU members is influenced by many variables.

- The term 'culture' encompasses the sum total of learned beliefs, values, customs, rituals, languages, symbols, artefacts and technology of a society or group.

- Different societies vary greatly in most aspects of culture, but all culture is social, learned, shared, cumulative and adaptive.

- Products can be invested with cultural meaning by marketing efforts; that meaning is transferred to a buyer who uses the product in a cultural context and hence imbues it with further cultural meaning. This is called transfer of cultural meaning.

- Marketing cross-culturally brings a number of new challenges. Two approaches can be used: localised markets (marketing a product so that it fits into the existing culture) or global marketing (capitalising on the fact that culture changes and develops, so a 'foreign' product can gain acceptance into different cultures in the same form worldwide).

- The marketing department of a supplier aiming at corporate clients needs to be aware of:
  - how buying decisions are made by the DMU;
  - how the DMU is constructed; and
  - the identities of the most influential figures in the DMU.

18 CONSUMER MODELLING   *16 mins*

You have been asked to investigate the potential for consumer modelling as a means of preparing a marketing plan for *either* a national lottery *or* a nationwide chain of fast-food outlets. Having selected one of these options, write a report summarising your views about:

(a) the general benefits of consumer modelling;

(b) the specific application possibilities for the product/service under consideration.

(10 marks)

19 TUTORIAL QUESTION: THE VALUE OF CONSUMER MODELLING

Whilst attending a conference, your Managing Director learns about consumer modelling from an enthusiastic speaker. The MD now believes that consumer modelling may yield some benefits for the organisation, but she still remains cautiously sceptical and has requested an input on the subject from you. Prepare a memo, in response to this request, in which you:

(a) explain what consumer modelling tries to do;

(b) outline its potential benefits and hazards in general terms; and

(c) evaluate at least two major approaches to consumer modelling with which you are familiar.

You may assume for the purposes of your answer that you work for either a global airline or an international hotel company.

Guidance note

Be warned! Parts (a) and (b) are relatively straightforward. When you are asked to evaluate two approaches to modelling in part (c), make sure that you do indeed critically appraise them, rather than limiting your answer to a description of their features. Relate your answer to your chosen organisation.

20 MODELLING BENEFITS   *16 mins*

What are the general benefits of consumer modelling? How should they be evaluated? What different types are available?   **(10 marks)**

21 PRICING PSYCHOLOGY   *16 mins*

Working for a large airline, you have been asked to review the prices charged for your product. Write some observations in response to the following questions (which can be assumed to be part of your brief).

(a) Discuss the psychological significance of price.

(b) Evaluate the potential economic consequences.   **(10 marks)**

22 ORGANISATIONAL BUYING CENTRES   *16 mins*

Give a definition of an organisational buying centre and discuss its influencing factors.

(10 marks)

23 BEHAVIOUR AND THE DIFFUSION OF INNOVATION   *32 mins*

Research has indicated that the diffusion of an innovation follows a normal distribution (a bell shaped curve) over time. What are the behavioural characteristics of the principal groups of customer occupying each segment of the distribution curve?   **(20 marks)**

In report format identify how you would gain access to, and influence, the 'innovator' or 'early trier' group if you were charged with the responsibility of promoting either a sophisticated new soft drink or a radically different concept in home entertainment.

(20 marks)

24   INNOVATION SUCCESS   *32 mins*

It is said that product innovation requires consideration of two issues.

(a) *Diffusion* - the 'macro' process by which the innovation is spread or disseminated from the source to the potential customers.

(b) *Adoption* - the 'micro' process by which the customer makes a decision to accept or reject an innovation.

What useful things could you say to your marketing director if he/she asked you to supply some input on both these issues relative to the possible introduction, by your organisation, of a radically new product or service?

You may choose to illustrate your material by reference to recent cases of new product/service innovations, such as Philips Digital Compact Cassettes or the Sony Mini-Disc.   **(20 marks)**

25   SPENDING RATHER THAN TALKING   *32 mins*

'Customers are most sincere when spending rather than talking', says Nishikawa. What is the significance of his view for:

(a) the supposed links between attitudes and behaviour; and

(b) the design of research aimed at assessing the potential for new products or services?

(20 marks)

26   PERCEPTION AND SETS   *16 mins*

What relevance do each of the following have for marketers?

(a) Subliminal perception

(b) The concepts of the evoked set, the inert set and the inept set in consumer evaluation of competing products.   **(10 marks)**

27   APPROACHES TO MARKET SEGMENTATION   *32 mins*

Approaches to market segmentation can be classified as follows.

(a) A *priori* segmentation - i.e. segments are identified prior to any market research being undertaken, or *post hoc* segmentation, where customers are grouped into segments on the basis of research findings.

(b) Segmentation according to *objective* variables (like quantity purchase, frequency of purchases etc) or *subjective* variables (such as degree of brand loyalty, life-style, etc).

If you were a marketing consultant, which approach or combination of approaches would you recommend, and why, for segmenting the actual/potential market for *either* an airline *or* a bicycle manufacturer?

Write your answer in the form of a report addressed to your client's board of directors.

(20 marks)

28 TUTORIAL QUESTION: SIGNIFICANCE OF SEGMENTATION

Your manager has just returned from a marketing lecture at which it was claimed, using the words of Yoram Wind, that customer segments should be 'measurable, accessible, substantial, and homogeneous in their responses to marketing variables'. It is clear that she has not fully appreciated the points being made, nor adequately recognised the significance of segmentation as a contributor to commercial success. Indicate how you would respond if she were to put these questions to you:

(a) What precisely is meant by the four factors mentioned by Wind as the essential characteristics for customer segments, and why is each of them so important?

(b) Why do so many organisations, in both consumer and industrial markets, fail to segment their markets successfully?

(c) What steps can organisations take in order to avoid making such mistakes?

Guidance note

This is a relatively straightforward question. Think about some of the causes of failed segmentation. Having up to date information on your customers is vital, so that you do not use outdated methods of classifying them.

29 CONSTRUCTING SEGMENTS   *32 mins*

Produce a systematic checklist showing the principles that should govern the construction of market segments. Illustrate your material with examples of segmentation systems relevant to various kinds of product/service and to various kinds of customer, both individual and organisational. **(20 marks)**

30 SEGMENTATION SYSTEM   *32 mins*

You are a marketing consultant retained by a construction firm that specialises in building residential accommodation of all kinds. Write a memo, as if to your client's Marketing director, incorporating these features.

(a) The benefits of customer/market segmentation.

(b) Your reasoned arguments for the segmentation system which would be most beneficial for your client. **(20 marks)**

31 THE DEATH OF SEGMENTATION   *32 mins*

A marketing lecturer has shown you an article she's written entitled *The Death of Segmentation*. The central argument in the article is that because customers increasingly expect to be treated as individuals, then grouping them together into 'segments' will be increasingly inappropriate for tomorrow's organisations. Invited to comment on the article, how would you respond? **(20 marks)**

32 ATTITUDES AND BEHAVIOUR   *32 mins*

What are the connections between 'attitudes' and 'behaviour' so far as customers are concerned? Amplify your arguments with references to relevant examples including, in particular, the possible impact on purchasing behaviour of customer attitudes toward environmental issues. **(20 marks)**

33   ATTITUDES AND PURCHASES   *32 mins*

It is well known that attitudes and behaviour do not always coincide. Using this assumption as the starting point, answer each of the following questions.

(a)   What are the reasons for the fact that, sometimes, favourable attitudes (towards a product) may not lead to significant purchases, whereas, on other occasions, unfavourable attitudes can nonetheless generate purchase decisions?

(b)   When designing some market research in order to test the potential for a brand new product, how would you seek to reduce the likelihood of drawing the (potentially false) conclusion that favourable attitudes towards the product would inevitably be translated into a corresponding number of purchases for the product?   **(20 marks)**

34   REASONS AND MOTIVES   *32 mins*

Why is it so difficult to find out the reasons and motives behind consumer purchasing decisions? Outline some of the methods used by marketers in an attempt to overcome these difficulties.   **(20 marks)**

35   MOTIVATIONAL THEORIES   *32 mins*

Several motivational theories were developed in the first place in order to describe and explain what motivates people *at work*. Outline any three such theories and examine their usefulness to marketers in explaining the behaviour of people as *customers*.   **(20 marks)**

36   PSYCHOANALYTICAL THEORY   *16 mins*

Psychoanalytic theory has been criticised for having little relevance to marketing because it deals with deep-seated needs and motives derived from childhood conflicts. For what type of product categories might psychoanalytic theory provide insights into consumer purchasing motives?   **(10 marks)**

37   DMU   *32 mins*

Write a memorandum to the marketing director of a major toy manufacturer in which you outline your views on each of the following.

(a)   The market segmentation systems which would be especially relevant for a toy manufacturer.

(b)   The relevance to your business of the distinction between 'customers' (people who pay for the product) and 'users' (people who use the product but who are not the purchasers as such).

(c)   The importance of understanding the other roles in the Decision Making Unit, and how your marketing activities might be influenced by them.   **(20 marks)**

38   TYPES OF GROUP   *32 mins*

There are several kinds of groups to which individuals may belong.

(a)   Ascribed groups and acquired groups
(b)   Primary groups and secondary groups
(c)   Formal groups and informal groups
(d)   Membership groups and aspirational (reference) groups

Explain what is meant by each of these terms and give examples to demonstrate their relevance to marketing.   **(20 marks)**

39   BUYER BEHAVIOUR   *32 mins*

You have been asked to deliver a presentation to a large marketing conference. Your brief is to suggest some criteria an organisation might use to decide which of the following would be the most effective way to market their products/services.

(a)   Globally
(b)   Nationally
(c)   Global marketing but adapted to local conditions

What points and arguments about buyer behaviour would you make in your presentation?

(20 marks)

40   SECONDARY GROUPS   *16 mins*

Define the following types of group.

(a)   Primary and secondary
(b)   Formal and informal
(c)   Membership and symbolic   **(10 marks)**

41   BUSINESS BUYING BEHAVIOUR   *16 mins*

What factors distinguish business customers from household or individual customers?

(10 marks)

42   RESELLERS   *16 mins*

Who is a reseller and what value does a reseller provide to end users?   **(10 marks)**

43   CUSTOMER IS KING (SPECIMEN PAPER)   *32 mins*

Critically examine the accuracy of each of the following statements which are often to be found in marketing literature.

(a)   'The customer is king (or queen).'
(b)   'The customer is always right.'

In what circumstances is it possible that these propositions could be successfully challenged?

How accurate are they, for example, when applied to (1) the concept of the 'internal customer' and (2) the 'customers' of a monopoly such as a water utility, municipal authority or taxation-funded central-government department.   **(20 marks)**

DO YOU KNOW? – INVESTIGATING CUSTOMER DYNAMICS

- *Check that you know the following basic points before you attempt any questions. If in doubt, you should go back to your BPP Study Text and revise first.*

- Information about customer dynamics is acquired in a variety of ways. Data is systematically collected and analysed to provide useful information. A detailed database about present and past customers, with details of the nature of the relationship; it has to know about their attitudes, their perceptions of the organisation's products and service, and their expectations is a useful tool in retention marketing.

- Nishikawa emphasised creativity and understanding customer psychology. His key point was that customers are most sincere when they are spending, rather than when they are taking part in surveys.

- Lele and Sheth proposed four fundamentals of customer satisfaction.
  - ° product-related variables
  - ° sales and promotion related variables
  - ° after-sales variables
  - ° culture-related variables

- Companies are likely to use a combination of qualitative and quantitative techniques when undertaking research.

- Sampling is a key topic in marketing research. Be aware of the various sampling methods.

- Customer responses may be affected by bias, or they may not respond at all.

- A key element of customer care is finding out what customers think and what they want.

- The main method of qualitative research is the interview.

- Projective techniques attempt to draw out attitudes, opinions and motives by a variety of methods.

- Focus groups concentrate on discussion of chosen topics in an attempt to find out attitudes. They do have limitations despite advantages such as the ability to observe a whole range of responses at the same time.

- There are several quantitative methodologies for measuring customer responses and perceptions.

- Be aware of good practice in relation to: questionnaire design, conducting interviews, conducting telephone surveys, postal surveys, experimental research, continuous research, in-home scanning, in-store testing and retail shop audit.

- The collection of secondary data is often referred to as desk research, since it does not involve the collection of raw data from the market direct. Desk research includes using library sources, the organisation's information system, databases and internal reports.

- Environmental scanning is an informal process resulting in the possession of market intelligence. Sources include newspapers, journals and attending conferences.

- Useful statistics are published by government and non-government sources.

- Data and reports can be bought in from marketing research organisations. Often these are the result of continuous research using consumer and retail panels.

- Secondary sources of data are of limited use because of the scope for compounding errors arising from why and how the data were collected in the first place, who collected them and how long ago.

- Customer and competitor intelligence are vital tools in any organisation's marketing strategy.

- Customer intelligence depends on understanding customer priorities, segmenting customers into differing expectation groups, and designing appropriate methods for the systematic acquisition of customer feedback.

- Relying on customer complaints as a source of evidence for measuring customer satisfaction is extremely dangerous.

- Securing information about actual and potential competitors can be achieved through diligent attention to secondary data.

- Secondary data can be cost-effective, but should be used with care.

44 TUTORIAL QUESTION: THE CASE FOR MARKET RESEARCH

Defend the case for commissioning market research to help reduce the risk of costly marketing mistakes.

Guidance note

This question covers the outcomes of market research, not the methods. Avoid making exaggerated claims as to what market research can achieve.

45 MARKET RESEARCH *32 mins*

If you were invited to give a talk to business studies undergraduates under the title, 'What Can Market Research Do? What Can't It Do?', what points would you make?

(20 marks)

46 MARKET RESEARCH METHODOLOGIES *32 mins*

(a) What are the respective merits and potential disadvantages of qualitative versus quantitative methodologies in the market research process?

(b) Which methods, or combinations of methods, would you advocate as a means of discovering useful data about the marketing potential for *either* (a) 'virtual reality' machines, (b) wall-mounted LCD television sets, (c) an electric town car, or (d) voice-recognition office dictation systems?

Produce your answer in the form of a *marketing consultancy report* and proposal to a marketing director. **(20 marks)**

47 PRIMARY AND SECONDARY RESEARCH *16 mins*

Use examples to explain the meaning of secondary research. Explain the limitations of using secondary research in practice. **(10 marks)**

48 PRIMARY AND SECONDARY DATA *16 mins*

Your firm wants to do some market research on the European market for a possible new product launch. You are a part of the marketing team undertaking the research. A colleague working in finance who is responsible for costing the project asks you how you intend to find out about the market. Your colleague has specifically asked for an explanation of the following.

(a) The meaning of the terms 'primary and secondary data' in the context of market research.

(b) How secondary date may be used and any advantages such data has over primary data.

(10 marks)

49 RESEARCH TECHNIQUES *32 mins*

There are a number of specific marketing research techniques that may be employed to research consumer behaviour. An airline you are advising on marketing research is concerned to find out the following.

(a) What influences a customer's choice of airline?

(b) Which services customers value highly and are prepared to pay a premium price for?

BPP PUBLISHING

Required

Write a brief report on the three specific research techniques that are listed below and explain the appropriateness of the techniques listed to achieve the stated research objectives. You should provide a brief but clear explanation of each technique and discuss how it may be used in this context.

(a)   Shopping mall tests

(b)   Focus groups

(c)   Postal questionnaires   **(20 marks)**

50   MOTIVATION RESEARCH   *16 mins*

Within marketing research, what is meant by the term 'motivation research' and what is its background? Explain psychodrama and give brief details of other methods available.

(10 marks)

51   INTERVIEWING METHODS   *32 mins*

Julie Roberts, a member of your marketing department, is about to conduct a number of interviews with users of a particular product that your company supplies. The particular researcher is as yet undecided on the specific research method to be used. Time and cost are obvious considerations and Julie has written you a memo asking for your advice on the suitability of telephone interviews as opposed to face to face. Julie is also concerned to establish qualitative data as part of the research and thinks it insufficient merely to provide quantitative summaries.

Required

Write a memo to Julie advising her about appropriate research strategies that should be considered in order to establish the qualitative data. Your memo should give clear advice about the relative merits for each approach mentioned.   **(20 marks)**

52   TUTORIAL QUESTION: CUSTOMER SATISFACTION

Set out a plan for a research programme to measure customer satisfaction for an organisation that has never systematically investigated such matters before. Illustrate your plan with reference to a named organisation of your choice and show how the results yielded by the study could be beneficial for your organisation.

Guidance note

The choice of 'named organisation' is likely to be important. It is worth spending a few moments thinking of a context which fits the requirement of the question ('never systematically investigated such matters before') but which is manageable in terms of size and complexity. Choosing Toyota or Tesco is likely to be both unrealistic and too demanding, hence our choice of a smaller enterprise (see Answer).

53   TUTORIAL QUESTION: DATA COLLECTION USING QUESTIONNAIRES

What are the different ways of collecting data using a structured questionnaire? What are the relative advantages and disadvantages of each method?

Guidance note

Set your answer out in a table format with columns for advantages and disadvantages.

54 RESEARCH SURVEY METHODS *32 mins*

Your Managing Director wants to undertake consumer research with the aims of finding out:

(a) how attractive your current product range is; and

(b) how attractive your prices are vis a vis competition.

In this context you are asked to write a memo to your Managing Director explaining the main types of consumer research survey methods and detail their relative advantages and disadvantages, bearing in mind the areas of the research. **(20 marks)**

55 TUTORIAL QUESTION: VALUE OF CUSTOMER SURVEYS

Your Marketing Director does not believe in customer surveys because, he says, the respondents seldom tell the truth. Write a memo to the Marketing Director in which you:

(a) Assess the justification (or otherwise) for his views.

(b) Show how methods for investigating customer perceptions can be designed in ways which enable the result to be regarded as acceptably accurate.

Guidance note

Do not ignore the requirement for a memo. Our suggested format is to set out the reasons why survey respondents may not always tell the truth, and then to suggest ways of overcoming the problems. Feel free to disagree with the Marketing Director's views if you can support your arguments.

56 SECONDARY SOURCES OF DATA *32 mins*

A well-established Japanese company is thinking of starting up an operation in your country but wishes to assess the commercial potential of your environment before committing itself. What are the principal sources of economic and business information, and other secondary sources of data, which may give the company a reliable basis for determining whether or not to proceed? (If you wish, you may specify the business sector in which the Japanese company specialises, eg financial services, pharmaceuticals, fast food, department-store retailing, or management consultancy.)

(20 marks)

57 MARKET INTELLIGENCE *16 mins*

You have been appointed to lead a marketing programme for a company, already well established elsewhere but now contemplating a sales/marketing drive in your country. Part of your role is to acquire market intelligence about your company's competitors. What methods could you use? Give reasons for your choice. **(10 marks)**

58 DATA COLLECTION *32 mins*

You are preparing to give a lecture to marketing students about 'Primary and Secondary Methods of Data Collection in Marketing Research'. Outline the structure of your talk and summarise the main points you would want to get across to your audience in the 60 minutes allotted to you. **(20 marks)**

BPP PUBLISHING

59 DATA FOR OVERSEAS EXPANSION
32 mins

You work in the marketing department of a US company that is contemplating expansion overseas. The company is currently in the data collection phase and the Marketing Director has asked you to identify relevant sources of information about some of the markets that your organisation may enter. Write a memo in response to your Marketing Director's request, discussing the types of date typically available and their value. **(20 marks)**

60 NEW PRODUCT RESEARCH
32 mins

A company is considering introducing a new alcoholic drink aimed at 18 to 30 year olds and wants to know:

(a) How the product will be received.
(b) How many units it can expect to sell in the first year.
(c) What price it should charge for the product?

Required

As the new marketing manager responsible for introducing the new brand, outline the steps you would need to undertake and any specific marketing research techniques you would employ in order to produce answers to (a), (b) and (c) in the form of a short report. **(20 marks)**

61 NEW PRODUCT MARKET RESEARCH
32 mins

You are newly appointed as a marketing manager in a publishing company and have been given specific responsibility for a new product launch. Your organisation wants to introduce a new magazine aimed at the teenage female market as identified as part of last year's strategic review. In this respect you have been given a budget of £30,000 to conduct further market research prior to the launch. Explain how you would plan and conduct this research. You are required to give the specific stages in your research plan and evaluate and justify each of your chosen options.

(20 marks)

62 PROJECTIVE TECHNIQUES
16 mins

Discuss the value of projective techniques in marketing research. **(10 marks)**

63 MASS CUSTOMISATION (SPECIMEN PAPER)
32 mins

Debates continue to range about whether mass customisation is (a) a marketing opportunity, (b) a threat, (c) a passing fad, or (d) an illusion. Imagine that you work for a car manufacturer: write a report for your Marketing Manager in which you comment on each of the four interpretations offered above, in the context of the motor industry, and offer a reasoned assessment of the benefits and risks associated with mass customisation so far as your own company is concerned. **(20 marks)**

64 ATTITUDE FORMATION AND CHANGE   *32 mins*

What are the principal theories about attitude formation and attitude change? Which of these theoretical perspectives might be relevant, and how could they be applied, in order successfully to change attitudes (and behaviour) in any one of the following scenarios:

(a) Persuading adults to drink (more) milk

(b) Persuading adult males to switch to a new type of shaving technology

(c) Persuading people to purchase items through the Internet

(d) Persuading young car drivers and their passengers to wear seatbelts

(e) Persuading smokers to abandon smoking altogether or to transfer to some form of nicotine substitute.   **(20 marks)**

BPP PUBLISHING

DO YOU KNOW? – CUSTOMER DYNAMICS AND THE FUTURE

- *Check that you know the following basic points before you attempt any questions. If in doubt, you should go back to your BPP Study Text and revise first.*

- There is likely to be continued enhancement of customer expectations in terms of: product/service quality (beyond functionality); organisational service standards and response times; and restitution processes (the 'aspirational customer').

- Customers now demonstrate intolerance of broken promises and impatience with delays and they transfer performance achievements experienced in one sector into expectations about performance delivery in another (the 'demanding customer').

- Customers have increasing opportunities to complain and willingness to do so, supplemented by legal enhancements to consumer power and the availability of media outlets (the 'litigious, complaining and powerful customer').

- Customers have concerns about ecological and environmental issues, about product/service ingredients and about ethical issues such as poor employment conditions in supplier organisations.

- Prompted by ever-increasing competition and constant attacks on costs, markets, profitability and resources, more and more organisations are redefining themselves to operate on a global scale.

- The world economy has been characterised by the rapid growth of service sector activities.

- The existence of a 'global consumer' is tied to the concepts of global standardisation and adaptability.

- The reasons for marketing overseas include a small domestic market and perceived opportunities to exploit economies of scale.

- Calculating the lifetime value of a customer can be done by roughly estimating the annual gross profit that they generate, working out customer retention rate and multiplying them together.

- Customers can be divided into three groups for communication purposes.

  - Potential customers
  - Customers who have made one purchase
  - Premium customers who have made more than one purchase

- Electronic commerce can broaden trade horizons and create wider markets for products and services.

- The Internet is affecting all businesses in similar ways. Every industry is now part of a global network, with all companies in the industry equally contactable. Information is now a more readily available commodity.

- Electronic commerce has eliminated many of the competitive advantages enjoyed by existing competitors and will affect the value chain by making some parts of it redundant, and creating entirely new delivery systems.

- To satisfy customers, manufacturers of the immediate future will require a fundamental shift in organisational cultures. To create value for customers, manufacturers, in other words, must eliminate traditional boundaries between customers and integrate more closely with them.

65 TUTORIAL QUESTION: DELIGHTING CUSTOMERS

'The customers who don't want choice and who don't want to be satisfied' was the challenging title of a recently published article. What the author meant was that customers today want products and services which are tailored precisely to their individual needs, and they seek 'delight' rather than mere 'satisfaction' from their purchases.

(a) How far do you agree that these are the emerging trends among customers in general?

(b) In your view how does this affect the future of customer segmentation?

Guidance note

Segmentation is regularly examined and this question presents a new angle on it, namely that segmentation into customer groupings will become less relevant as customers are targeted individually and increasingly come to expect the personal touch. Try to include relevant real life examples in your answer as this will impress the examiner. He often comments that students do not show enough awareness of current issues.

66 CHANGES IN CUSTOMER BEHAVIOUR AND EXPECTATIONS *32 mins*

Imagine you have been asked to give a presentation on the ways in which customer behaviour and expectations may change over the next ten years. Outline your notes for this presentation, in which you propose to address three principal themes.

(a) Changes in the marketing for existing products and services
(b) The appearance of new products and services
(c) The disappearance of some products and services currently on offer **(20 marks)**

67 TUTORIAL QUESTION: TRENDS IN BEHAVIOUR

In addressing the requirements for this question, you should firstly imagine yourself to be employed by an organisation in *any one* of the following fields: world-wide airline travel, telecommunications, package holidays, car manufacturing, book publishing, classical music compact discs, financial services, fast food, or sports-shoe marketing. You should then produce answers to these questions (as if they have been put to you by your marketing director):

(a) What are the major five developments or changes in customer behaviour which, in your view, are likely to have a significant impact on your chosen organisation over the next few years? You should supply a brief explanation to accompany each point being made.

(b) What steps do you believe the organisation should take, both to capitalise on the favourable trends and to offset the negative consequences of the unfavourable ones.

Guidance note

Note that the question specifically asks for examples of developments or changes in customer behaviour, so make your choices fit the demands. Choose the scenario/industry with which you are most comfortable/knowledgeable. Otherwise make sure you follow the instructions for each part. Avoid unsubstantiated waffle about trends in customer behaviour. Try to present cogent arguments for the premise that customers are going to go on wanting more, with previously acceptable standards of performance being overtaken. Then state how organisations could take advantage of such developments.

68   TQM AND COMMITMENT   *16 mins*

At a meeting, you hear your Chief Executive say that 'If we're serious about our commitment to customers, then we must have Total Quality Management in place.' Write a memo to the Chief Executive, commenting on the necessity of a link between 'commitment to customers' and 'Total Quality Management'.   **(10 marks)**

69   TQM AND CUSTOMER SERVICE   *32 mins*

Write a report, as if addressed to your management team, discussing the merits and weaknesses of the statement (taken from a marketing text) that "Several organisations appear to have pinned their entire hopes for future success on customer service and/or Total Quality Management; they believe that, by offering more service and more quality, they will create competitive advantage and customers will flock to them". Ensure that your report incorporates some recommendations appropriate to the future of customer service and/or TQM as sources of competitive advantage.   **(20 marks)**

70   DATABASES AND RELATIONSHIP MARKETING   *32 mins*

Information technology is improving the ability of retailers to capture, store and retrieve a variety of data. As a sales and marketing manager with responsibility for retail promotions, explain in a short report for other functional managers how you propose to use new technology to track customer promotions and achieve your objective of increasing sales volumes over the next year. In particular, explain what information technology is available and how you propose to use it for competitive advantage.   **(20 marks)**

71   COMPLAINTS PROCEDURES   *16 mins*

Consumer dissatisfaction may result in a complaint. Discuss the key aspects of consumer complaint behaviour.   **(10 marks)**

72   ENVIRONMENTAL ISSUES   *16 mins*

In your opinion, in which area have the environmental issues had the biggest impact on consumer behaviour?   **(10 marks)**

73   SOCIAL TRENDS   *16 mins*

Is the political consumer a fad or a new and growing challenge for marketers? Discuss.   **(10 marks)**

74   NEGLIGENT CONSUMER BEHAVIOUR   *16 mins*

Define negligent consumer behaviour and identify four examples.   **(10 marks)**

75   DELAY MANAGEMENT   *16 mins*

How can organisations seek to minimise consumer dissatisfactions caused by delays?
                                                                            (10 marks)

76 ELECTRONIC COMMERCE (SPECIMEN PAPER) *32 mins*

You are the newly-recruited marketing officer for either an international airline, a newspaper publisher, or a holiday package-tour business.

Produce a memo for your company's marketing department in which you explore:

(a) The future for electronic commerce in general terms.

(b) The implications so far as your own organisation is concerned. And

(c) A reasoned set of actions which you believe your company should take in order to capitalise on the opportunity or prepare itself for the threats. **(20 marks)**

77 DEMANDING / ETHICAL CUSTOMERS (SPECIMEN PAPER) *32 mins*

'Customers are becoming more aspirational, more demanding, more litigious and more ethical, all at the same time', you hear someone say at a marketing conference. What do these claims mean, and what evidence could you produce to support them? Assuming that the speaker's predictions are correct, what are the implications of these developments so far as effective consumer marketing is concerned? **(20 marks)**

78 CUSTOMER SATISFACTION AND CUSTOMER DELIGHT (12/99) *32 mins*

You are the Marketing Officer for EITHER a large hotel OR a car dealer. Produce a report for your company's Head of Marketing in which you explore:

(a) The differences between customer 'satisfaction' and customer 'delight'.

(b) The reasons why it is so important to create the sensation of 'delight' among your customers.

(c) The ways in which it could be done.

Illustrate your arguments by examples relevant to your chosen organisation, i.e. the hotel or car dealership. **(20 marks)**

79 CUSTOMER 'ISSUES' (12/99) *32 mins*

It is claimed in a recent publication that 'Customers...are no longer acting like rational, economic entities. They are swayed by political, ethical, ecological and other 'issue' considerations'.

Imagine that you are employed in the Marketing Department of either an electricity supply company, a package holiday firm or a global bank. Write a memo for your Manager in which you assess the accuracy of the quotation above and explore its implications (in terms of marketing strategies) for your own business. **(20 marks)**

80 MINI-CASE: FAST-FOOD GROUP (SPECIMEN PAPER) *64 mins*

The PleasureFood Restaurant Group

As the name of the company suggests, the PleasureFood Group operates a collection of fast-food restaurants located principally in town and city centres, shopping malls, leisure complexes, and airports. The Group has expanded from a single café/bar opened by the PleasureFood company's owner about 30 years ago; it now has 75 units, some run directly by PleasureFood's personnel, and some operated by franchisees.

The PleasureFood strategy has been founded on organic growth, but it is now contemplating more rapid expansion, if promising lines of development can be found. Some of the major alternatives include: diversification into food 'manufacturing', industrial catering (ie restaurants inside office buildings for corporate employees), the creation of branded food products for sale through supermarkets, and entry into overseas markets.

Each of the PleasureFood restaurants is built to a common standard and is intended to provide identical meals and service. Head Office supplies detailed instructions about every aspect of the PleasureFood operation, including portion control, cleanliness and hygiene, the appearance of the staff, the words and phrases used when communicating with customers, and price/product standardisation.

Currently, Pleasure/Food's principal customer segments are teenagers, shoppers, and families with children. It has around 30 per cent of its chosen market place, its major competitors being McDonalds, Burger King and a couple of the major pizza companies; the remainder of the competition is occupied by very small, local companies.

The PleasureFood group is a well-managed and successful company. It is in good shape financially. However, the Board consists entirely of people who have spent their careers with PleasureFood, and Board meetings are dominated by the presence of the company's owner.

Required

You are a consultant who has been engaged by PleasureFood's Marketing Director in order to offer the company some guidance about the optimal direction which it should pursue in the future. Produce a report initially aimed at the Marketing Director but ultimately intended for distribution to the Board, in which you respond to each of the issues raised by the Marketing Director in her brief, as follows.

(a) Given the fact that the PleasureFood Group has never established a customer database, and has never systematically investigated customer perceptions about its products and service, how could it cost-effectively acquire such a database and also secure definitive information about customer satisfaction? **(10 marks)**

(b) What are the major trends in customer segmentation and customer dynamics which could affect the PleasureFood Group's business in the foreseeable future?

(10 marks)

(c) Assuming that one of the options facing the PleasureFood Group is expansion into overseas markets, what are the factors which should be evaluated before such an option is actively pursued? **(10 marks)**

(d) How could the PleasureFood Group create competitive advantages for itself against the major threat presented by McDonalds? **(10 marks)**

Note: It is permissible to make assumptions by adding to the case details supplied above, provided the essence of the case study is neither changed nor undermined in any way by what is added. You may assume that the PleasureFood Group is located in the UK or in any other country of your choice. **(40 marks)**

81   MINI-CASE: PRINTING COMPANY (12/99)   *64 mins*

Platinum Print

Platinum Print is a privately-owned company, with the majority of the shares held by John Rush; the other shareholder is his brother, but he plays no active role in the business. The Board consists of John Rush (as Managing Director) plus three Executive Directors responsible for Operations, Marketing/Sales, and Finance. Established in 1970, the company now has around 80 employees; it has grown very slowly but now stands poised, potentially, for more spectacular expansion because it has acquired a bankrupt competitor.

The equipment used by Platinum Print enables it to print in a maximum of two colours (plus black); its machines are fairly old and the company's profit margins have not been sufficient to justify their replacement. Platinum's field of expertise is concentrated in such products as 'café pads' (the note pads used by waiters and waitresses in restaurants for taking customer orders), invoice books, envelopes and standard or customised office stationery.

Customer segments

Four-fifths of Platinum Print's sales are conducted through stationery supply companies, both wholesale and retail; the remaining 20% is fragmented among a number of direct clients, such owner-operated restaurants, small fast food chains, and family businesses of various kinds (egg in retailing, distribution and the building trades). The vast majority of the firm's customers are located within 50 miles (80 kilometres).

Competition

Printing is a highly competitive business. Overall, the market is static or in decline, as organisations become capable of in-house document production through desktop publishing equipment, and as companies communicate increasingly through electronic media rather than by conventional correspondence. Many of the items in Platinum's 'catalogue' are distress purchases (ie customers order them as a matter of necessity rather than because they want to). Winning orders, in what is virtually a commodity marketplace, is widely seen as being dependent on price. No single competitor has more than a very small share of the total sales in printing.

The current situation

You have been engaged by John Rush to re-energise the Platinum Print business and capitalise on the opportunities generated through the acquisition of its bankrupt former competitor.

Required

Produce a report for the Managing Director of Platinum Print, John Rush, in which you supply responses to the following four issues which he has put in front of you.

(a) At present the company has no systematic mechanisms for obtaining, analysing and acting on customer feedback. Outline the methodological options available and indicate (with reasons) the approach you would recommend to Platinum Print, given its current customer profile.   **(10 marks)**

(b) John Rush has heard of relationship marketing and thinks that it may offer some opportunities for his company. Briefly summarise the generic rational for relationship marketing and assess its potential for Platinum Print.   **(10 marks)**

(c) Platinum's employees are immersed in the crafts of printing, typesetting, typographical design and other technical skills associated with the company's operation. In the view of John Rush they display insufficient concern for customers. What could be done to

27

encourage them to be much more customer focused, so far as the company's external clients are concerned? **(10 marks)**

(d) At present, Platinum Print has no particular competitive advantage which differentiates it from other printing companies. How could it create one? **(10 marks)**

Note: It is permissible to make assumptions by adding to the case details supplied above, provided the essence of the case study is neither changed nor undermined in any way by what is added. **(40 marks)**

Answer bank

1   **CUSTOMERS AND USERS**

> **Tutorial note.** The solution to this question is presented in point format. Remember that the examiner gives marks for supplying an answer in report format if that is required, and also that you were asked to address only one of the scenarios.

To: The Marketing Department
From: A. D. Visor
Date: December 2000

CUSTOMERS OR USERS?

Definition of customers. A person who pays for the product/service.

Definition of user. A person who uses the product.

The two definitions are not mutually exclusive, but where they are separate people they need to be separately targeted. This is because the user's needs and reasons for wanting a product will be different to the customer's.

Toy manufacturer

User: child; customer: parent, adult friend. Children are of great influence in the purchase decision but ultimately it is the adult's. Appeals need to be to both parties: convince the child that it is a desirable product, convince the adult that it is educational and value for money.

Car retailer

	Users	Customers
Company purchase:	Staff	Fleet Manager
Private purchase:	Family members	Male partner (typically)

Two separate messages need to be conveyed for company purchase in particular. To the user, the retailer needs to market the car's comfort, speed, style etc. To the customer, the message needs to be about value for money, reliability, trade-in value, and discount.

2   **KNOWING AND UNDERSTANDING THE CUSTOMER**

In some market segments it is possible for an organisation to know its customers extremely well - for instance, a mechanical engineering firm may only have four or five large customers. But to know someone is not necessarily to understand them, especially when the customer Decision Making Unit is very complex, as it would be in this example. In the consumer market, furthermore, it is not possible even to know all customers, let alone understand them.

Marketers address these problems by undertaking marketing research, which includes soliciting and analysing feedback from existing customers. Even so, the information gathered tends to be either historical or hypothetical: for instance, finding out what the customer has bought in the past (a fact) and what he or she intends to buy in the future (a hypothesis at best). In fact customers are very volatile, changing attitudes and intentions very rapidly in response, say, to an innovation from a competitor or a scare story in the press. Suddenly what the marketer knew or understood has become meaningless.

A further problem is that marketing research does not succeed at **predicting** customer behaviour (although statistics can be helpful in demonstrating how likely there is to be an error in information extrapolated from historical data). This is because of the nature of customers: when presented with a hypothetical scenario ('would you buy this thing you've

BPP
PUBLISHING

never seen if you had the money?') they can give answers which are vain and self-deluded, irresponsible, impulsive, ignorant and ingratiating. The scenario is artificial and so there is no just cause to treat the answers as objective information. So while historical data can be analysed to give useful and verifiable information, provided conditions which existed in the past seem set to continue into the future, marketing research for new products is based on hypothesis and so can be notoriously misleading.

Whether to go ahead with a product launch can be researched using experiments and surveys, but ultimately many successful innovations have been launched on a 'gut-feeling', against the 'objective' evidence. A proven example of this is the Sony Walkman: research showed that people did not want a cassette player that did not record, but failed to highlight the fact that customers do not always know what they want until they are given it. The launch went ahead, and the rest is history.

3   CONSUMER POWER

The primary concern of consumerism is to ensure the consumers' rights in the exchange process. These include the right to be informed, to be told the truth, to be given adequate alternatives and to be assured of health and safety in the process of consumption. These activities have come to be known as the consumer movement.

There are three types of organisations that make up the **consumer movement**.

(a) Consumer-oriented groups concerned primarily with increasing consumer consciousness and providing customers with information to improve their basis for choice eg Friends of the Earth.

(b) Government through legislation and regulation eg Advertising Standards Authority.

(c) Business through competition and self-regulation.

Various studies have been conducted to help determine the **reasons for increasing awareness** of consumer rights. Findings include the following.

(a) Greater concern regarding advertising to children.

(b) Greater awareness of the potential for misleading advertising eg health and beauty claims.

(c) Increasing consumer awareness of social problems, particularly relating to the disadvantaged and to the environment.

(d) A feeling that the concern of business should go beyond the maximisation of profits to encompass social concerns.

Marketing organisations have a responsibility to ensure each of the aforementioned consumer rights are addressed. The question is whether marketing will accept these responsibilities in the interest of furthering self-regulation or whether they will relegate these responsibilities to government in the expectation of further legislation, more controls and the establishment of more regulatory bodies.

The preference in a marketing society, on both pragmatic and ideological grounds, is for self-regulation rather than additional government regulation. However there are still indicators of the need for continued government controls eg the failure of large companies to immediately recall unsafe products and the pollution of the waterways by the chemical industry.

4 CUSTOMER ORIENTATION

The principles of customer behaviour serve a company best when they are applied to developing and maintaining a customer orientation. Customer orientation means a thorough understanding of customers' needs and wants, the competitive environment, and the nature of the market, and is used to formulate all of the firm's plans and actions to create satisfied customers.

When firms and organisations become customer oriented, they reap gains. First, they gain a significant **competitive advantage** in the external market place. Second, internally, they are able to cultivate **satisfied employees** who feel pride in their jobs. Employees are an organisation's internal customers. Through customer orientation, then, the firm is able to offer value to both internal and external customers.

Following a customer orientation will provide a company with competitive advantages that lead to **higher corporate performance** in the form of increased profitability and revenue growth. There are six advantages, three of which increase profitability and three that generate revenue growth. The three advantages that increase profitability are cost efficiencies from repeat customers, price premiums from established customers and customer loyalty in corporate crisis. The three advantages that generate growth are increased word of mouth, one stop shopping and new product innovations.

Furthermore, customer orientation creates **pride in employees**. This is especially true for the front-line employees if they experience job satisfaction. Front-line employee satisfaction depends greatly on the extent to which they are able to satisfy their customers. The influence also flows in the opposite direction. Happy customers lead to employee happiness. Grudging, complaining, dissatisfied customers actually take a toll on employee morale.

5 CUSTOMER VALUE AND PROFITABILITY

There are a variety of issues surrounding the statement and these will now be discussed in bullet point format.

- Profit maximisation is not always an organisational goal. For example non-profit and government organisations are likely to have different objectives (eg awareness creation).

- Nonetheless, these organisations are likely to have customers and hence the reference to superior customer value may still apply (eg providing services to those with particular needs).

- These two criteria suggest that accurate measurement is possible and this may not always be the case. Individuals in organisations perform a variety of functions, some of which are measurable (eg productivity) and others that may be more difficult to determine (eg service quality in teaching or the police force).

- Individuals within organisations are employed principally to achieve corporate results and not simply to perform tasks.

- The statement would appear to discourage innovation and risk taking - key aspects of many successful organisations (eg 3M).

Occupational roles

The role selected is that of a research and development scientist, in the context of a pharmaceutical organisation. Such individuals are recruited on the basis of their qualifications, their previous experience and successful project developments. Pharmaceutical products can be many years in development and then take several years to

BPP
PUBLISHING

reach the market place due to the required trials needed to determine effectiveness. As such it would be quite possible for a scientist to work for decades without making any contribution to profitability. Indeed the individual is likely to be a cost as they will be salaried and will require laboratory equipment etc. If a successful product is launched which alleviates a medical condition then superior customer value is likely to result.

If these two parameters were to be forced on a scientist, then there is the potential for a number of outcomes. Innovation could be stifled as imitative products will have a faster development cycle and so are likely to have a faster return on investment. However, superior customer value is likely to be affected as the organisation may fail to develop products that offer sustainable competitive advantage.

In conclusion this statement could be said to be selectively accurate, dependent on the organisation, its aims and objectives and the role of the individual.

6   TUTORIAL QUESTION: RELATIONSHIP MARKETING

Perhaps the most talked about concept in the field of marketing is relationship marketing. Relationship marketing can be defined as the overt attempt of exchange partners to build a long-term association in which purposeful co-operation occurs, mutual dependence occurs and social, as well as structural bonds, are developed.

In many respects, the relationships that result resemble marriages. As in marriages, organisational relationships move through a series **of stages**.

(a)	Awareness of each other	First meeting
(b)	Exploration	First date
(c)	Expansion	Going 'steady'
(d)	Commitment	Marriage
(e)	Dissolution	Divorce

As in marriages, managers in the organisational buying centre must recognise that give and take will exist with suppliers. Similarly, the sales force must be willing to adjust rapidly to the changing needs of its customers. Managers must recognise that, as in marriages, the dissolution phase will be much more difficult than in traditional contractual exchanges.

Another critical element in building long-term relationships is trust. Relationship trust can be defined as a willingness to rely on an exchange partner in whom one has confidence. Thus, to reveal trust in a relationship, the members must reveal vulnerability to each other. In such cases, control of important resources is left with the other member of the exchange. As a result, the exchange members must rely on each other to fulfil their obligations in the exchange. When high levels of trust exist, the exchange process becomes more flexible and less bureaucratic, and legal entanglements are minimised.

7   BRAND EQUITY

From the customers' point of view, brand equity is the value of that brand to the customer compared to other brands. More formally, brand equity may be defined as the enhancement in the perceived utility and desirability that a brand name confers on a product. It is the customer's perception of the overall superiority of a product carrying that brand name compared with other brands.

There are five **dimensions of brand equity**.

(a) **Performance** - a customer's judgement about a brand's fault free and long lasting physical operation and flawlessness in the product's physical construction.

(b) **Social image** - the consumer's perception of the esteem in which the consumer's social or reference groups hold the brand.

(c) **Value** - the brand's perceived utility relative to its costs, based on a comparison of what is received and what is given up.

(d) **Trustworthiness** - the customer's trust the brand has won - trust that the brand will maintain its strengths, and that it will not compromise its quality or otherwise take advantage of its customers.

(e) **Identification** - the degree to which customers identify themselves with the brand or feel some attachment to it. In effect, consumers would say that it is their brand. It is the kind of brand they would be happy to be associated with. Often, identification occurs because the brand is associated with things, persons, and ideas or symbols that individuals find engaging.

8 TRUST AND COMMITMENT

Trust and commitment underpin relationship-based buying. For a customer to be engaged in relationship-based buying at all, the customer has to trust the marketer and then make a commitment to the marketer.

The most essential ingredient in any relationship, whether business or social, is trust. If there is no trust, there will be no commitment, it is from trust that relationship-enhancing behaviour spring. **Trust** can be defined as a willingness to rely on the ability, integrity and motivation of the other party to act to serve needs and interests as agreed upon implicitly or explicitly.

Long-term customer relationships are also characterised by commitment, that is, an enduring desire to continue the relationship and to work to ensure its continuance. In household markets, for example, a customer who is committed to their phone supplier would not switch suppliers just to gain a temporary price deal

In business markets, **commitment** is not merely the carrying out of certain contractual obligations (such as a reseller displaying the product according to the manufacturer's written requirements); rather, it requires making every effort to promote the partner's business. To continue the reseller example, rather than simply give the product display at the stipulated location and the amount of shelf space, the retailer proactively thinks up ways of giving the product maximum possible exposure. The commitment manifests in co-operative behaviours, but it goes beyond individual acts of co-operation. It refers to a mind-set of pledging to do nothing that would harm the relationship and doing everything needed to nurture it.

9 STAFF MOTIVATION

Herzberg asked a sample of professionals about circumstances affecting their satisfaction and happiness at work. From their responses, he developed the well-known two factor theory of motivation. In this a distinction is drawn between:

(a) Satisfaction in the sense of a positive, conscious state of happiness.

And

(b) Satisfaction as a neutral state reflecting an absence of negative sensations.

For example, many individuals take good health for granted and are therefore satisfied until they become ill.

Herzberg classified the positive satisfiers as motivators while the neutral version (or potential dissatisfiers) he refers to as maintenance or hygiene factors. His studies suggest the following:

Hygiene maintenance factors	Motivators
Company policy/administration	Achievement
Supervision	Recognition
Salary	Work itself
Interpersonal relations	Responsibility
Physical working conditions	Advancement

The theory suggests that the presence of dissatisfiers causes low work performance, so the maintenance/hygiene factors must be put right. However this does not lead to motivation, only to the 'no dissatisfaction' type of satisfaction. Motivation, and hence high work performance, is generated by the motivators.

It should be noted that the maintenance factors are commonly extrinsic to the job and the motivators intrinsic. The work can be criticised on a number of grounds, not least that it was based on a relatively small sample of engineers and accountants in America. However it has had wide acceptance in the organisational setting.

If Herzberg's work were to be replicated in the UK in 1999, it is possible that the results would be different. The world has become increasingly materialistic with house prices and the general cost of living increasing. A multitude of factors influence motivation in the work place. These include job security and the aforementioned factors. Undoubtedly money does have a significant role for most employees but it needs to be considered in conjunction with other factors.

10   VALUE FOR CUSTOMERS

Value delivery has two dimensions, **effectiveness and efficiency**. Effectiveness is the ability of the product or service to meet the customer's needs and wants. Efficiency is minimal cost to the customer, measured in money, time and physical effort to receive that value. The less a product or service costs, the more efficient it is from the customer's point of view.

If a marketer's offering fulfils a customer's needs and wants very well, and if in obtaining and using that offering the customer has to expend as few resources (time, money, and physical effort) as possible, then both efficiency and effectiveness are being simultaneously harnessed to achieve the best value for the customer.

For example, if the marketer offers the customer a better product (which implies higher effectiveness) at a lower price or at greater convenience (ie at a higher efficiency), then the marketer has created the best possible combination. However, if a company can offer a better product but only at a higher price, or if it charges a low price but cannot offer good quality at that price, then the accrued value is only partial. Therefore, the ideal goal of a marketer ought to be to leverage both effectiveness and efficiency to deliver the best value.

In the business-to-business service markets, Federal Express offers value both via effectiveness and efficiency. It offers effectiveness by satisfying customer need for on time, guaranteed delivery of time-sensitive documents and packages. On the efficiency side, it conserves the customer's time and effort resources via its collection service and via giving customers computer software so they may process the shipping themselves.

However, its price value is no better then its competitor's. Business firms also offer efficiency value to customers by providing access via the internet so that customer effort is interacting with the firm is minimised. Firms that offer electronic document delivery such as a database or a journal article offer both effectiveness and efficiency - having the information on electronic medium allows customers to use that information more effectively, for example, via word search, or cutting and pasting, enhancing the graphics and photos etc.

11 CUSTOMER SERVICE ENVIRONMENT

A shop's atmosphere delivers a message to consumers, such as 'high quality clothes for the more mature customer' or 'trendy clothes for the young clubber'. Atmospherics is a more general term than shop layout, it deals with how organisations can manipulate the design of the building, the interior space, the layout of the aisles, the texture of the wall and floor coverings, the smells, use of colour as well as the sounds experienced by customers.

(a) **Merchandise**

This refers to the actual goods themselves and also the way in which they are arranged. There is a movement in the grocery sector to group products together. So instead of the salad and the salad dressing being four aisles apart, they are placed together to encourage purchase. The layout of the shop can impact on the duration of the visit. A shop that is messy and disorganised is likely to be off putting.

(b) **Service**

The expectations of service levels differ between sectors. For example, in the grocery sector, the understanding is that most consumers know what they want and where to find it and so customer service levels are low. More exclusive department stores pride themselves on the expertise of their staff who will be happy to spend time helping shoppers with their purchases. These service levels may include free delivery, a generous returns policy, ordering facilities, exclusive sales events and so on. These benefits will be supported by a premium pricing policy.

(c) **Clientele**

The vast majority of clothing retailers target specific segments. As such one would not expect to find someone over 30 in Top Shop nor an individual who was a size 10, in Evans. This issue refers back to the issue of self-image. Most individuals have some idea of what they look like and more importantly what they want to look like, hence the importance of attractive window displays. If, upon entering a clothing shop, an individual sees people who are like themselves, or how they would like to look, then they are much more likely to enter.

(d) **Promotional activities**

These need to be appropriate to the target market. More upmarket retailers will hold seasonal sales to allow for the new seasons clothing to be displayed. It is likely that these will be held on a regular basis eg summer and New Year and their clientele are likely to be familiar with this. Shops which hold sales outside these established times are sending out signals. Perhaps they have misjudged the market or bought unwisely and so find themselves with excess merchandise which they need to dispose of to address a cash flow issue.

(e) **Atmosphere**

When the atmosphere arouses the consumer and positive emotions already exist, the buyer tends to spend more time in the shop and has an increased tendency to affiliate with people. A chain of bookshops is experimenting with comfortable seating and refreshments in-store. The idea behind this is that if customers can spend a few minutes sitting comfortably reading the first few pages of a book, then they are more likely to purchase it. Researchers have proposed that atmospherics is becoming increasingly important as the number of competitors increases, as the differences in product and price decrease among the competitors and as the market becomes more and more segmented.

12 THE SERVICE ENVIRONMENT

The design of the service environment is an important aspect of service positioning strategy and sharply influences consumer impressions and consumer and employee behaviour. The physical environment is particularly important in creating a favourable impression for services such as banks, retail stores and professional offices. The reason being that there are so few objective criteria by which consumers can judge the quality of the services they receive. The service environment conveys the image of the service provider with whom the service is so closely linked. Thus at private banks, expensive mahogany desks, leather chairs and opulent décor project stability, solidity, wealth and power.

The Polo/Ralph Lauren store in the renovated 1895 Rhinelander mansion in New York is the embodiment of the image Lauren wants to create for his clothes: traditionalism and old world values. All the trappings of what one imagines to the high-class ways of the very rich are here, from the baronial, hand-carved staircase lined with family portraits to the plush sitting rooms with working fireplaces. The Polo store image artfully extends the image of the clothing it sells, and projects an old world quality of living and shopping that its upmarket target market finds appealing.

One study of service environments identified the environmental variables most important to bank customers.

(a) Privacy (both visually and verbally such as enclosed offices, transaction privacy).

(b) Efficiency/convenience (transaction areas that are easy to find, directional signs).

(c) Ambient background conditions (temperature, lighting, noise, and music).

(d) Social conditions (the appearance of other people in the bank environment such as customers and bank personnel).

(e) Aesthetics (colour, style, use of materials, artwork).

Clearly a positive service environment creates the perception among consumers that the service itself better satisfies their needs.

13 TECHNOLOGY

In terms of customer behaviour, technology is the dimension of market context that consists of the applications of new technology to the development, distribution and consumption of products and services that increase the quality of life for all customers. Technological breakthroughs can significantly change market behaviour and customer expectations.

Advances in technology affect customer behaviour in four different ways.

(a) **Increased access to information technology** brings new mass media into being in the form of media that offers customers information about the marketplace. The role of conventional mass media is bringing market information to customers has been remarkable. The increasing acceptance of the Internet is likely to affect all business sectors. It can be used to buy a car, book a holiday, find out information on university courses etc. The information is global, as is access.

(b) **Product innovations** - the second aspect of impact of technology on customer choices is via the availability of new products and services based on advances in technology. The advent of Cable TV, especially with it's multi-channel offerings, and services such as pay per view and video on demand, will obviously impact on cinema audiences and video rentals.

(c) **Flexibility and control** - technology also affects customer behaviour by delivering freedom from the confines of space and time. That is to say, business can be conducted any place, anytime. ATMs (automatic teller machines) can be accessed 24 hours a day. Individuals can shop from home using the Internet or can order from home shopping TV stations. As customers can use technology to access any seller anytime, anywhere, distance or time no longer limits their choices.

(d) **Customised products and services** - one of the most exciting technological developments in recent years is in the manufacturing area, namely flexible manufacturing. The marketing benefit of technology is mass customisation producing a product after the customer order is received, and tailoring the product to the customer's specific needs without sacrificing the speed or cost efficiencies of conventional mass production methods. As such, mass customisation allows the firm to produce a product or service for a single individual customer in order to match their individual preferences, and do so nearly at the same low costs of assembly line production. For example, Hallmark uses computer technology to offer custom-made cards using computerised kiosks in shops. By using simple on-screen instructions, customers can choose from a selection of graphics, write their own message and instantly print the card, all for little more than an off the shelf card.

14 CUSTOMER SERVICE IN MANUFACTURING

To satisfy customers, manufacturers of the future will require a fundamental shift in organisational cultures. To create value for customers, manufacturers must eliminate traditional boundaries between customers and integrate more closely with them. This new state of manufacturing, where companies are expanding into new markets, confronting new competitors and coping with new technology, means that power and presence today does not guarantee power and presence tomorrow. New wealth from manufacturing is being created more by adaptability, value-added services and speed of execution than by sheer quantity of capital or machinery.

Differentiation in the era of the virtual customer will require superior marketing and customer service. Most manufacturers do not yet possess these capabilities. A global manufacturing study by Deloitte consulting in 1998, involving 900 executives in 35 countries, suggests that many continue to focus on product quality and neglect the integration of manufacturing with marketing and sales. While manufacturers say they recognise the importance of superior service, they have not kept pace with rising customers' expectations and tight delivery deadlines dictated by complex manufacturing systems.

To succeed in the next few years, manufacturers will focus on service-related attributes, such as:

- On-time delivery
- Customer-perceived product quality
- Prompt handling of customer complaints
- Fast response deliveries
- Building superior customer relationships

Ten days before it launched the 1995 Range Rover, Rover sent 10,000 of its most privileged customers invitations to a champagne breakfast or candle-lit dinner to see the new car privately – before the national launch. Those who attended were not expected to enter into an immediate commitment, instead the aim of the exercise was to inspire these individuals into becoming brand ambassadors for Rover.

The underpinning idea behind Rover's approach was **relationship marketing**, turning ordinary customers into brand advocates. In a relationship approach marketers endeavour to develop and build long term, trusting, win-win relationships with valued customers, distributors, dealers and suppliers.

Relationship marketing can be seen as the successor to mass marketing and is the process by which information about the customer is consistently applied by the company when developing and delivering products and services. Developments are communicated to the customer, for example via specially targeted promotions and product launches, in order to build a partnership with them and encourage long term relationships by paying attention to their specific needs. This is particularly true of fast moving consumer goods. Retailers are no longer solely responsible for their promotion and manufacturers are developing databases so that customers can be contacted directly.

The case of **General Electric** demonstrates some of the problems and opportunities arising from the unavoidable application of information technology to commerce and business. In recent years, GE has changed its core competencies completely and has transformed itself through a vision of more and more services, driven by providing useful information to customers. This presupposes that GE is able to discover what information its customers will find useful, and will then be able to invent some means through which the information can be collected, analysed, assessed and subsequently delivered to the customer in a usable form.

GE can provide services to help customers use their assets better, the locomotive division, for instance, sells software that enables customers to manage the routing on their railways more efficiently. GE plans to develop a capability that will allow it to keep track of all the modifications and changes made to everyone of its heavy-engineering products, so that it can assemble a complete history of each item. This in turn permits the company to offer more knowledgeable and expert advice when required; it too ties the customer more closely to GE, especially if it turns out that GE knows more about the customer's equipment than the customer does.

From the above illustrations and discussion, it can be seen that manufacturers are currently involved in developing customer service programmes and establishing relationship marketing as part of their business activities. It seems obvious that they are part of the tools available to a manufacturer to help them gain competitive advantage and as such are likely to increase in importance, as markets become more competitive.

15 CUSTOMER-CENTRIC ORGANISATION

When applied to the structure of an organisation, customer-centric means ensuring that issues such leadership, recruitment, reward systems, values, processes geared around customer types and so on, are all focused on developing and improving the level of customer satisfaction.

Features of an organisation that is not customer-centric – it is anticipated that an effective response to this section of the question would name a specific organisation and offer a rationale as to why they were selected. Several examples to illustrate the ways in which they are not customer-centric should be offered. For a retailer this could include concentrating on defending sales margins or discouraging feedback from lower levels. For the financial sector this could include slow rate of technological change and lack of product flexibility.

The response to the last part of this question, changes that would need to be introduced, will be specific depending on the organisation selected. Here are a few general comments:

- Link individuals in an established network of relationships so that authority, responsibility and communication can be controlled

- Group together the tasks required to fulfil the objectives of the organisation, and allocate them to suitable individuals or groups

- Give each individual or group the authority required to perform the allocated functions

- Co-ordinate the objectives and activities of separate units

- Facilitate the flow of work, information and resources

To conclude, a customer-centric organisation will focus on meeting the needs of customers and the development of structures and processes that will assist in achieving this aim.

16   CHANGES IN THE DELIVERY OF CUSTOMER SERVICE

There are a variety of factors that have contributed to this prediction. These include the shift to **electronic commerce** where there is limited personalised communication and the increase in global pricing as we see the development of the global village. These developments, along with comparative Internet sites means that customers can search for a product, for example a book, and be presented with a list of suppliers, prices and delivery times. As such pricing is unlikely to be the means for sustainable competitive advantage.

Organisations are constantly seeking to reduce costs through **automation**. For example IBM improved the Frequently Asked Questions section of its web site and reduced support costs by over $100million. By using technology for handling low-level customer-service activities, more time can be used for high-value, personal support.

Such developments have clear implications for organisational **structures**. Options may include delayering, downsizing and outsourcing. Increasingly organisations have begun to concentrate on what they see as the core activities of their business and so have outsourced their non-essential activities. This has been a spur to the growth of facilities management, since it has led to the contracting out of key services e.g. cleaning, recruitment and training. Downsizing has had the same consequences.

During the series of privatisations which took place in the 80s in the UK, many sections or functions within large companies were encouraged to set up as separate external enterprises, providing what were often intermittently needed functions such as plant maintenance and market research. The costs of staffing, training and managing such functions on a long-term basis were removed, and the function could be fulfilled on a competitive basis. Other sorts of services such as catering and security began to be filled in the same way.

Some organisations have endeavoured to reduce the physical, human interaction aspect of their business. Some supermarkets are offering customers the opportunity to scan their own purchases so there is no requirement to have to unpack them, have them scanned by a checkout operative and then re-pack them. Financial services such as Smile (Co-Operative Bank) have embraced Internet technology and offer products purely on-line. Such organisations are often referred to as customer-centric because they are organised in teams around specific segments of customers.

17   ENCOURAGING INNOVATION

DISCUSSION DOCUMENT

To: L. Aggard, Marketing Director, Dull Products Ltd
From: G. Ogetter, Marketing Consultant, Doit Ltd
Re: Action points from previous meeting
Date: 6th December 2000

Introduction

The following report has been written in response to out last meeting. You expressed concern regarding your organisation's inability to create new products and services. In addition, you felt that a key issue was your slowness in bringing new products and services to the marketplace as compared to your competitors. The purpose of this document is to provide a basis for discussion at our next meeting. As such it will focus on what you could do to create an organisational climate that is characterised by innovation and speed.

Characteristics of innovative organisations

Much research has been conducted on the nature of innovative organisations, however a key theme of all this research is that for organisations to grow or even survive, they must have plans for innovation. The chief objective of being innovative is to ensure the organisation's survival and success in a dynamic environment. An innovative organisation can exhibit some of the following organisational characteristics:

- Fostering individuals who are highly motivated

- Taking a proactive perspective and actively seeking challenges and opportunities

- Consistently challenge employees, setting ambitious goals and targeting thoroughly investigated and lucrative markets

- Creating a corporate culture that encourages new product/service development

- Recruiting, training and motivating creative people with clear rewards for innovation

- Delegating authority and responsibility so that ownership is established and morale and performance improved

The encouragement of innovation should result in the creation of a more outward looking organisation. This means that individuals are encouraged to look for new products, services, processes etc. and hence improve productivity. Here are some practical ideas that should encourage innovation:

- An innovation training programme so that all employees understand what it is and how it happens

- Ensure that appropriate financial support is available for R&D, market research etc.

- Encourage feedback from employees and customers regarding new ideas

- Develop multi-functional project teams

- Initiate quality improvement activities such as the establishment of quality circles

- Review recruitment, training and motivation policies in line with innovation encouraging strategies

- Develop innovation champions who will be responsible for obtaining information from outside the organisation about innovative ideas and will be responsible for its internal communication

All of the above suggestions need to be underpinned with a consistent and comprehensive strategic planning process. This should result in targets being set for innovation and successful achievements by employees should be appropriately rewarded.

Conclusion

The above report has highlighted and addressed the key issues currently facing your organisation. I look forward to discussing these with you at our next meeting.

18 CONSUMER MODELLING

> **Tutorial note.** Your answer should be in report format, and focus on one only of the organisations stipulated. You need to provide a rationale for why you have chosen the one you did. Our answer is in note format.

(a) **Benefits of consumer modelling**

Modelling allows us to 'map' or describe how customers behave and make decisions, so that we can attempt to predict and influence their behaviour. In particular, it allows us to isolate the factors that combine to create behaviour, and so can be a useful starting point for designing marketing research.

(b) **Evaluating a consumer model**

A good model should be valid, factually accurate, rational, complete, simple, original and effective for its purpose. A model can be:

(i)   Micro or macro.
(ii)   Descriptive, diagnostic or predictive.
(iii)   Low-medium-, or high-level.
(iv)   Static or dynamic.
(v)   Qualitative or quantitative.
(vi)   Data- or theory-based.
(vii)   Behavioural or statistical.
(viii) Generalised or ad hoc.

The Price PV/PPS model should be particularly appropriate to the products under examination.

19 TUTORIAL QUESTION: THE VALUE OF CONSUMER MODELLING

INTERNATIONAL HOTELS Inc.

To: M/s Dee Light, Managing Director
From: Anna Ministrator
Date: December 6 2000

Consumer modelling

(a) **Introduction**

The consumer modelling approach is based on the assumption that we can simplify the consumer buying process and illustrate this in such a way as to portray something useful and meaningful about the phenomenon. They may work at the level of understanding and explaining behaviour or even more usefully they may help us to predict consumers' actions.

Models can be of all shapes and sizes, the text books suggest that they can be verbal, algebraic or pictorial; micro or macro; descriptive, diagnostic or predictive; static or dynamic; qualitative or quantitative; date based or theory based; behavioural or statistical; generalised or ad hoc; simple or complex.

The language sounds impressive, complex and academic - but the reality is that we all have models built into the way we see the world and the way we make decisions. So if we interpret the academic language and just say 'if we cut the price, we will fill more rooms' this is, in fact, a workable model of consumer behaviour.

The CIM suggest that models can be evaluated on their validity, factual accuracy, rationality, completeness, simplicity, originality, heuristic power, explanatory power, predictive power. What is rather more important is how good the model is at doing its job.

(b) **Potential benefits and hazards**

If we use a 'good' model and benefits are self-evident if it actually allows us to predict consumer behaviour. But even if it cannot fulfil that particular function it may be of considerable use in:

(i)   Identifying key decision points.
(ii)   Planning campaigns.
(iii) Devising market research projects.
(iv)   Preparing advertising material.

The downside of models is that they may over-simplify the situation and so fail to be comprehensive with the inevitable hazard of missing a key element. Such a happening could lead to the generation of false or misleading conclusions, plans and, ultimately, financial loss.

(c) **Comparison of approaches**

Models are classified as:

- Black box
- Personal variable
- Decision process
- Comprehensive or 'grand'

The simplest format is the black box model - so called because it considers the consumer as an impenetrable black box. In other words it is concerned with inputs and outputs. Our earlier example of the linkage between price and buying behaviour would be a good example of a black box approach. Its advantages are its simplicity, its ability to be understood, and its obvious link to the real world of hotels. Its disadvantages lie in the same simplicity and the lack of insight into the processes that may mediate behaviour.

At the other end of the spectrum lies the Engel, Kollatt & Miniard model which is a comprehensive model. It is basically a problem solving and decision making model, concerned with need recognition, search, evaluation, purchase and post-purchase outcomes. However, part of its strength is a concern for other influences both environmental as well as individual differences between customers - thus allowing better planning. In our situation it would encourage us to consider factors such as:

- Culture
- Social class
- Family

As environmental aspects of the purchase of hotel accommodation, while other individual concerns such as:

- Knowledge
- Lifestyle
- Demographics

It could be invaluable in decisions concerning both specific product developments and the selling and marketing of them.

I hope these comments help to clarify your concerns regarding their usefulness.

20 MODELLING BENEFITS

Benefits of consumer modelling

A model, in this context, is a representation of consumer behaviour. The aim of models is to provide a simplified portrayal of consumer processes to help us in the task of describing, explaining, predicting and, ultimately, controlling buying behaviour.

The best parallel is that of a map. A model is a map of consumer behaviour, a framework we can use to understand what is going on, or to predict what will happen. The map analogy works quite well in the sense that if we are setting out to explore an area or a town or city, it helps to have a map. Some people have a well developed sense of direction - they seem to be able to find their way around surprisingly well - but even they may miss some important parts. As for the rest of us we may just blunder around looking, but having little idea of what or where we are.

A major problem is that we all have our own implicit, unwritten models of consumer behaviour. We 'know' how people react. The main problem is that we are often mistaken. As professionals we need 'maps' to find our way around - and not miss anything of importance!

In order to achieve this there are some widely accepted criteria for the evaluation of models. They should be:

(a) **Simple,** to aid understanding.
(b) **Factual,** to relate to reality.
(c) **Logical,** to be both understandable and plausible.
(d) **Original,** to contribute something new.
(e) **Valid,** so that their contribution can be verified.

In addition it is commonly accepted that good models have **explanatory power** and should generate ideas for further investigation (**heuristic power**).

There are a number of different types of model.

(a) **Black box** models focus on the inputs to the situation, but do not consider the internal variables or the processes through which a consumer may go.

(b) **Decision process** models follow the stages of decision making.

(c) **Personal variable** models concentrate on internal variable such as attitudes.

(d) **Comprehensive or grand** models seek to map the whole complex processes involved. Examples of grand models would be the Engel, Blackwell and Miniard model which identifies need recognition and motivation, information search, alternative evaluation, and finally decision making. The Howard-Sheth model, in contrast, uses inputs, perceptual constructs, learning constructs and outcomes.

In other words, we have a variety of models to choose from. Some take a macro view of the process, others a micro, individualistic perspective. Some are theory based, others are based on facts, data and observation. Some are behavioural, some are statistical. Some static, others dynamic.

In summary, the choice may lie between a simple, black box, model which is easy to understand but which may lack detail (for example, put the price down and we will sell more) or the comprehensive model which may cover many more elements but which may be unwieldy in use.

21 PRICING PSYCHOLOGY

(a) Psychological significance of price

The psychological significance with regard to the customer in terms of price is largely based on the perceived 'value for money' received from the service. One significant element in the airline scenario is likely to be the consideration of who exactly the customer is. The notion of 'value for money' may have very different dimensions when we are looking at solo travellers who are paying their own fares than the dimensions which may emerge when we look at business travellers whose flights are being paid for by their employers.

Of course, the customer may have had to work out as part of their decision the alternative methods of travelling, but following their decision to use our airline, they will be looking for overall satisfaction with the service provided. The customer will consider the level of comfort, whether travelling First Class, economy etc, and the actual service both on board, checking in and out and attention given during the journey. All this in addition to price.

Whether the customers find the service relaxing and a pleasing experience is of importance to them. However, the notion of 'value for money' will also depend on their perception of the price charged. From general studies of perception we know that a great deal of what we perceive is a function of the comparison with the environment, so we will need to look competitive relative to the immediate alternatives. Additionally we are all aware of the psychology of pricing 'below the zero' - £299.95 **seems** a lost less than £300.00 (the January sales syndrome).

(b) Economic consequences

The psychological impact can relate to ticket prices and this, in turn, can influence economic performance. If the 'economy' ticket is deemed by customers as better value for money, without much difference in service and comfort, more tickets in this class will be sold with implications for the 'luxury' class sales. On the other hand, business people or other travellers wishing to use the 'luxury' class may still perceive this class to be better value for money than using 'economy'. If there are two classes, both must be perceived as giving value for money in their own respective rights, and although levels of service, comfort and attention may differ within the two 'class' distinctions, customers must be happy with the overall service given and price they have paid.

Package deals and late bookings will most likely bring the feeling of value for money because of the reduced rate in the ticket price but this must be of utmost importance when reviewing charges.

The pricing policy is, in practice, likely to be influenced by a number of factors other than perception.

(i) The organisation's strategic objectives - for example we may be aiming to establish our presence on a particular route.

(ii) The overall marketing strategy - for example we may be aiming for a marketing mix which keeps price high and emphasises superior service.

(iii) Time of year - prices rise for Christmas and school holidays (supply and demand).

(iv) The elasticity of demand - we may wish to raise prices, but we may lose sales as a direct result.

22 ORGANISATIONAL BUYING CENTRES

An organisational buying centre is defined as those people in an organisation who participate in the buying decision and who share the risks and goals of the decision. Individuals within an organisation who frequently participate in a decision include managers, engineers, marketing personnel, finance staff and purchasing agents.

The same behavioural factors (ie psychological, sociological and anthropological) impact on buying centres as on consumers. However, as an organisation differs from a family in terms of its mission and its situational environment, there are divergent factors impacting on both groups.

The following table compares and contrasts organisation buying and consumer buying across six dimensions:

Dimension	Organisational buying	Consumer buying
Product	More technical, greater quantities, services offered	Less technical and more standardised, smaller quantities
Price	Competitive tendering, list prices on standard items	Generally buy on the basis of list prices
Promotion	Information from sales personnel and trade publications	Mainstream media
Distribution	Short channels, direct from manufacturer	Longer channels, retail or mail order most common
Customer relations	More enduring and complex	Transaction specific and simple
Decision process	People with diverse needs lead to more structured decision making	Fewer people involved and so unstructured process

23 BEHAVIOUR AND THE DIFFUSION OF INNOVATION

Tutorial note. The first part of the question is straightforward and your answer will benefit from the inclusion of a diagram to illustrate the stages of adoption of an innovation. The second part is more challenging - do not forget the report format and stick to the requirements of the question. Your recommendations should reflect the characteristics of the group as described in part (a). We have gone for the 'home entertainment' option in our answer.

The diffusion of an innovation is based on the work of Rogers who observed that the innovation is adopted by different groups of consumers at different stages temporally. This is commonly displayed via the 'bell shaped curve' referred to in the question:

'**Innovators**' are the first group who experience the process. These people tend to be:

• Relatively young

- Specialists in the field (ie are interested in the field, are always aware of industry developments, in particular via considerable exposure to media such as specialist magazines)

- Well educated

- Possess relatively high disposable income

- Venturesome in their purchasing habits, above all

'**Early adopters**' are the next consumer group for adoption. They are also quite highly educated and also have an interest in the industry's developments. Rather older, they do not rely on media sources so much for information on innovations as they are inquisitive and tend to search for themselves (not least by observing the innovators). They are 'sociable people' and are often seen as 'opinion' leaders' who pass on their comments to the following adoption groups. Marketing experts target them, as their 'positive' comments are a major weapon and tool.

The next group, the '**early majority**', are average in their level of education. They rely on the general media to bring innovations to their attention. They too are fairly sociable people.

The '**late majority**' are the next group and are rather below average in terms of education and income levels. Older, they, as do the early majority, represent about 34% of adopters. They learn of innovations from the 'early majority' from socialising.

'**Laggards**' are the last group (16% of adopters) and are adopting at a time when the innovators are using the next innovation. They are low on money, education, and knowledge of technological developments, are typically older and do not socialise very much.

So, overall, as we progress through the sequence, the members of those groups tend to be of diminishing social class, diminishing disposable income, diminishing interest in innovation. They tend to increase in age, but decrease in education and venturesomeness as the groups follow on.

REPORT

To: A. Golfer, Marketing Director
From: T. Off, Marketing Manager
Date: December 2000

Targeting Innovators for the 'Domestic Golf Experience'

Introduction

I have recently drawn up plans to identify 'innovators' for the launch of our new product the 'domestic golf green' and here are my ideas for identifying the people to target and how to communicate to them.

Findings

As you know, the 'domestic golf experience' is a machine which can be situated indoors and recreated the experience of putting on a golf course. The machine has a flat bed that adjusts to different gradients in order to test the average golfer (or professional if in difficult mode). It is ideal for the home.

As outlined above, innovators tend to be young, interested, higher class, high disposable income, exposed to specialist media individuals. To target such a group I would therefore suggest that we use appropriate role models/opinion leaders who could include:

- Golfing professionals

- Golfing coaches
- Research and development specialists from golfing manufacturers such as Ping, Calloway and Titleist
- Designers of golf courses

Recommendations

(a) That we arrange a demonstration event and invite members of the above. Agents may need to be contacted.

(b) Advertising and publicity via suitable specialist magazines such as Golfing Weekly - special features could be produced to tie in with the demonstration events outlined above.

(c) Competitions with the product as the prize organised via these media to capture names and addresses of actual innovators/enthusiasts

(d) The innovators will be influenced using the MIA technique and its criteria. Therefore we will influence them with positive messages for the products:

- Relative advantage
- Compatibility
- Complexity (simplicity)
- Trialability
- Observability

Conclusions

The above listing of innovators are deemed appropriate for our new product. This report will be followed by details of the launch dates and innovators involved/present.

24 INNOVATION SUCCESS

I should tell my Marketing Director that the concept of innovation is very much a perceptual phenomenon - ie it is what is seen as 'new' that matters.

Rogers suggested that there are five characteristics that are associated with the success of new products and the macro diffusion process. They are as follows.

(a) **Relative advantage**

This is the extent to which a consumer perceives the product to have an advantage over the product it supersedes. Clearly logic suggests that the greater the perceived advantage, the greater the probability that the product or service will catch on.

(b) **Compatibility**

This makes the assumption that the less a product is compatible with the consumer values, the longer it will take to be adopted. This could also apply to the extent to which the technology is compatible with that which the consumer is both experienced and comfortable with.

(c) **Complexity**

The more complex and difficult it is perceived to be, the harder it will be for the product to be accepted.

(d) **Trialability**

Here Rogers suggests that new products are more likely to be adopted when consumers can try them out on an experimental basis.

(e) **Observability**

This characteristic is a measure of the degree to which adoption of the product, or the results of using the product, is visible to friends, neighbours and colleagues. This seems to affect the diffusion process by allowing potential consumers to see the benefits of the product, and thus increase (or even create) a 'want' for themselves.

There may well be additional factors.

(a) The **time lag** before consumers experience the desired benefits (in such cases the prediction would be that the greater the delay in gratification, the less the chance of trying out the product).

(b) The **symbolism** of the product for the consumer seems to be another important factor - how else can we explain the dominance of Levi jeans when they are so very similar to most others jeans?

(c) The **reputation** of the organisation can also be a helping influence - it is often asserted that IBM computers are not as technically advanced as many of their competitors. Their products continue to dominate the market because of the reputation the company holds and the fact that to many people computers mean IBM.

Innovators are venturesome individuals who are willing to take risks.

Early adopters are often viewed as more respectable but are quick to take up new ideas that they have seen 'piloted' by the innovators. They also seem to act as some sort of role models and opinion leaders for the …

… **Early majority** who, typically, may seek to avoid risks and who are relatively deliberate in their purchasing behaviour. While the …

… **Late majority** are sceptical and cautious about new ideas and the …

… **Laggards** are very traditional and set in their ways.

The time dimension is important as the model suggests that each group learns by observing the previous group's behaviours and then, after the 'vicarious learning', adopting the behaviour itself.

The characteristics of these consumer groups has been the focus of a great deal of research. The results suggest that innovativeness is often most clearly marked in people who are of high social status, upwardly mobile, educated and/or literate and young. But, not surprisingly, on of the key determinants is income. High income people not only have the ability to buy more new products, they also have the ability to risk trying new products. This factor is likely to be of extreme importance when dealing with high cost items, but the linkage when considering low cost, low involvement goods is less clear.

Some research has indicated personality variables - innovators are more likely to be risk takers. Other research has proposed a possible link between innovation and cognitive style of problem solving - innovators being people who tend to produce different ways of organising, deciding and behaving which may involve significant change and the undertaking of new activities.

Communication patterns also appear to link with innovation. Earlier adopters seem to use both mass media and interpersonal sources more than later adopters.

25 SPENDING RATHER THAN TALKING

> **Tutorial note.** Don't get too thrown by the quotation - focus on the two questions set.

'Actions speak louder than words.'

'Words are cheap.'

'Put your money where your mouth is.'

These are all everyday expressions (or clichés) which are of relevance to the Nishikawa quotation.

The implication is that people do not always tell the truth when asked questions by a market researcher and Nishikawa makes the point that the only moment that you can really trust a consumer is when they actually part with money and commits themself to a purchase.

A similar example (although no money was exchanged) occurred during the run up to the 1992 General Election in the UK. The opinion polls had the Labour Party well in the lead and predicted a significant victory for them. In the event, however, they lost the election and the Conservative Party was re-elected for another term in office. The pollsters were embarrassed by inaccurate predictions caused by the public saying one thing but doing another. The soul searching which followed suggested that people responded to questions by saying what they thought was the 'right' thing to say.

(a) Sometimes this is an offshoot of wanting to be politically 'correct' or subscribing to the general, popular view (perhaps an element of peer group pressure).

(b) Sometimes this is because of wanting to please the questioner.

(c) Sometimes this is to reduce dissonance (the feeling of unease) when being asked for opinions.

Attitudes/behaviour linkage

It is generally accepted that there is a link between attitudes and behaviour and that the linkage is two way, often displayed as follows.

$$\text{Attitude} \leftrightarrow \text{Behaviour}$$

This implies that attitudes influence behaviour but that behaviour (our experiences) also influences attitudes. However, it is not always as straightforward as this.

Attitudes have three components.

(a) Cognitive (understanding and belief).
(b) Affective (feeling of liking or disliking).
(c) Conative (the behavioural tendency).

It can be argued that asking people for their opinions in a market research exercise is likely to be better for assessing the first two components than the third. This may account for the often-observed gaps between the attitudes which people express and what they actually do. There are a number of reasons for this.

(a) **Economic.** Jack has a very positive attitude towards Ferrari motor cars - but there is little chance of him ever being rich enough to afford one.

(b) **Time lapse.** Attitudes change over time. The gap between being asked something and doing something may be long enough for Sally to change her mind because of things such as…

(c) **New information**. Mike's response may have been honest at the time but new information has come to his attention. (He used to smoke once upon a time...)

(d) **Values change**. Many people originally thought that producing test-tube babies was wrong - but the passage of time has led to a general acceptance of the technique.

(e) **Conservativeness**. Nancy may say that she is interested in a new brand of baked beans - but when it comes to shopping she falls back on the trusted old favourite.

(f) **Control**. Life (and decisions) may be influenced by the things that are outside of one's control (weather, illness and so on).

Implications for marketing research

This discussion highlights some of the problems inherent in collecting attitudes towards products or services and expecting the findings to accurately predict subsequent behaviour. The traditional marketing research approach of asking people questions in order to forecast whether or not they are likely to purchase a particular product, vote a particular way or join a specific pressure group clearly has some limitations.

A major problem is that everybody finds it difficult to give honest, realistic answers to hypothetical questions. It would not be surprising to find an overwhelming majority of respondents answering 'yes' to a question such as 'would you be interested in buying an economical, environmentally friendly vehicle, suitable for town use which is easy to park and which runs on clean rechargeable electrical batteries?' Yet the Sinclair C5 was one of the great marketing disasters of recent years because customers reacted negatively when they saw what the product actually looked like.

A possible solution to this problem is to involve potential customers in a product's design a development process. Such customer panels are customer trials which involve the respondents in 'real life, hands-on' experiences which should allow them to make more reliable and realistic predictions about their behaviour.

Another developing area for some ranges of products allows actual purchasing patterns to be identified for individual households. (The Sainsbury and Tesco loyalty cards linked with EPOS technology allows much more detailed information to be collected on people's actual purchasing behaviour. Working back from this and using, for example, psychographic profiles, better predictions of future behaviour may be made from analysis of the past.)

26   PERCEPTION AND SETS

(a) **Subliminal perception**

There is an absolute threshold level of stimulation, below which there is no sensation at all: the exact level will vary according to an individual's sensitivity and circumstances. However, this appears to lie below the threshold ('limen') of conscious awareness or recognition: individuals can receive certain stimuli which are too weak or too brief to be consciously seen or heard: this is 'subliminal perception'.

Interest in subliminal perception was aroused in the late 1950s by the ethical issues surrounding subliminal advertising. It was claimed that consumers were being exposed to messages that persuaded them to buy certain goods, or act in certain ways, without being aware of seeing the messages, and without knowing why they subsequently acted as they did. Public protest at such supposed manipulation aroused academic interest.

A six week test was reportedly carried out at a drive-in cinema in the USA. 'Eat popcorn' and 'drink Coca-Cola' were flashed on-screen during the movie, so quickly that they were not consciously 'seen' by the movie-goers. Sales of both products increased over the trial period, but there was no control group to verify the reason for the change.

The evidence of subsequent laboratory experiments suggested that:

(i)   individuals could perceive below the threshold of their conscious awareness; but

(ii) they could probably not be persuaded to act in response to such stimulation (eg to buy a given product).

(b) **The concept of set**

Howard and Sheth formulated a model to show how 'set' works in consumers' brand choice.

(i)   There will be some brands of which the individual will not be aware at all. This unawareness set will not impact on his decision.

(ii) There will be some brands of which the customer is aware - his awareness set - and from which he will make his selection.

(iii) Within the awareness set, there will be a group of brands which he will call to mind and consider purchasing. This is called the evoked set.

Also within the awareness set, according to other writers, there may be:

(i)   an inert set of brands, of which the individual is aware, but about which he is completely indifferent. (Perhaps he has insufficient data to make a judgement - or perhaps the evoked set of brands are already sufficient for his needs); and

(ii) an inept set of brand of which the individual is aware, but about which he is negative - because of bad past experience, associations, reports or whatever.

Sets are of relevance to the marketer because:

(i)   they represent consumer perceptions - a relevant indicator of a product's position and competitors;

(ii) they dictate strategies aimed at raising the profile of a product (if it is in the unawareness set), encouraging evaluation (if it is in the inert set), or improving product/image (if it is in the inept set).

27   APPROACHES TO MARKET SEGMENTATION

Date: December 2 2000
From: P. Edal
To: Squarewheels Cycle Company
Subject: Segmentation of markets

Introduction

Segmentation is the process of breaking down a broad and varied market into groups. Successful segmentation results in sub-groups which **differ significantly** from each other in their requirements, but which are large enough to make it profitable to develop separate marketing or product offerings. In a successful segmentation exercise the sub-groups should also be **accessible** and **identifiable** as well as being **measurable** and **stable**.

The idea of segmenting the bicycle market is of prime importance to an organisation seeking to target customers. Your market is made up of many different kinds of customers and it is important for you to know who these customers are and how to sell the products to them. Segmentation holds the key for you and successful bicycle sales.

A priori or post hoc segmentation

In a priori segmentation segments are identified in advance of any market research while in post hoc segmentation the segments are determined following research and based upon it.

Advantages of a priori segmentation

The advantages of this approach are that it is relatively cheap and quick. We sit down in advance and decide which groups we are going to target - in the case of the cycle market we might decide to 'go for' segments based on age (children, adult, commuters, adult off-roaders) and as you can see such a decision could be made very swiftly.

Disadvantages of a priori segmentation

The great weakness of this approach is the danger that we get the segments wrong - or, even more likely, fall into the trap of assuming that, for example, all off-roaders are the same. In other words a priori segmentation is limited by the imagination and knowledge of the persons making the priori decision.

Advantages of post hoc segmentation

Post hoc segmentation has the advantage of starting with a relatively clean sheet and a relative absence of preconceptions. It is possible to undertake research specifically to identify groups which satisfy the characteristics of successful segments as listed above (ie different, sizeable, identifiable, measurable, accessible and stable).

Disadvantages of post hoc segmentation

It is likely to be time consuming, expensive and may not identify any segments which were not evident to experienced observers of the market already.

Segmentation by objective or subjective variables?

This classification draws a distinction between segments based on hard, objective data such as purchasing patterns derived from existing sales figures, and subjective variables based on less tangible aspects such as life-style or benefit derived from purchase.

Advantages of objective segmentation

The main benefit of objective segmentation is its relative certainty - if we are operating off of age, or purchasing pattern we are dealing with known variables.

Disadvantages of objective segmentation

The objective data may not be relevant. In the case of bicycles it is unlikely that there will be any significant pattern of bicycle purchase as most people buy bikes rarely. We may also have to consider the fact that many or even most purchasers of children's bikes are parents or adults - and hence the picture can become even more confused.

Advantages of subjective segmentation

This acknowledges that the motivation of purchasers may be emotional and varied. In the case of cycles the benefit sought could be of a number of different types - some seek fitness, others want cheap transport, some wish to pose while yet others may wish for an excuse to wear lycra shorts in public

Disadvantages of subjective segmentation

The notion of lifestyle may prove difficult to isolate and target in segmentation terms.

Conclusion

In the context of the cycle industry, I would recommend a mixture of a priori and subjective segmentation. The a priori approach will encompass a degree of objective analysis - age, socio-economic grouping, postcode etc while the subjective will concentrate on the crucial lifestyle aspect which is likely to prove the most potent segmentation tool of all. This should ensure the most effective coverage of the significant sections of the bicycle buying public without engaging in expensive and time consuming research to establish who might be worth targeting with lifestyle analysis. Hence we obtain the most useful analysis at least cost.

28   TUTORIAL QUESTION: SIGNIFICANCE OF SEGMENTATION

I would respond by prefacing my comments with a few words about the importance of segmentation to marketing and emphasising that attempting to approach the whole market is both inefficient and unrealistic. Market segmentation involves breaking the total market down into groups that we might target for existing products or develop products and services specifically to meet the particular needs of the segment. So segmentation may be used to either identify a segment and address it in order to sell existing products or services or alternatively it could be used to identify the product/service needs of a significant group and thus enable the development of products for that segment.

(a)   The characteristics of a successful segment identified by Wind might be clarified as follows:

Accessible: this is concerned with being able to reach the individuals making up the segment. It may be relevant in three contexts, firstly we need to be able to reach the members of a segment in order to carry out market research, secondly to reach them with our marketing messages and lastly, at a later stage, we also need to be able to reach them with the product or service.

Substantial: here Wind is emphasising that the segment needs to be large enough to support the effort required to investigate and market to it. This ties in closely with the need to provide goods and services profitably.

Homogeneous: the whole point of identifying a segment is that the individuals making up the segment should have some characteristic in common, this will enable the marketer to make use of the segment effectively.

Measurable: implicit in all of the above characteristics is the need to be able to measure the segment in terms of size and characteristics.

It may also be useful and relevant to note that there are some other characteristics which may be significant - these include the notion that the segment should be **stable** (at least to enable access as described above to take place) and perhaps even more importantly it should be **different** or **unique**. This is important, as the aim is to avoid overlap when identifying and exploiting segments.

(b)   There are a number of possibilities to explain why so many organisation, both in consumer and industrial markets, fail to segment successfully.

(i)   As society changes, organisations may be clinging to segmentation systems which were useful in the past but which are no longer so relevant. Relying heavily on class for segmentation purposes might be an example of this type of error.

(ii)   Organisations may fail to understand the true nature of their business which may lead to the construction of segments based on inadequate or wrong assumptions.

(iii)   Failing to realise that consumer market segmentation systems may not be relevant or effective in industrial markets where the number of potential customers may be significantly smaller, and all potential customers may be both identifiable and contactable.

(c) The ways in which organisations can avoid making such mistakes stem largely from the observations in part (b).

   (i) Organisations need to conduct relevant, up-to-date research to ensure that decisions are based on sound data.

   (ii) Managers need to be open-minded and treat decisions seriously and originally to avoid the danger of the 'we've always done it this way' trap.

   (iii) They need to be aware of latest thinking in the marketing literature and research in case new ideas are evolving which could be of use in their particular situation.

They could also profitably call in consultants who have specific segmentation expertise to advise them on the most relevant and appropriate systems.

29 CONSTRUCTING SEGMENTS

Introduction: segmentation

Except in a very small, specialised market (or, alternatively a monopoly situation), it is unlikely that any organisation will be able to serve total a market. Thus the need to carve the market up into segments becomes an important strategic decision for the enterprise.

The advantage of segmenting a market is twofold - firstly to prevent the firm attempting the impossible, and secondly to split the total market up into groupings each of which can be investigated to identify the needs, wants and problems which are specific to that group.

Ideally, the total market should be divide into segments which maximise the **difference between** groupings and which maximise the **similarity within** each segment.

If this is achieved the marketing specialist can devise marketing messages which are targeted specifically at the different groups.

Criteria and principles

In segmenting markets, key **criteria** are that they should have these characteristics.

(a) **Substantial**: is it sufficiently large to warrant niche activity?

(b) **Viable**: will it be profitable? The fact that a segment exists does not necessarily guarantee it can be served profitably.

(c) **Sustainable**: interest should be on long-term success. Will it dry up after a few years?

(d) **Accessible**: can the inhabitants be reached? If insufficient distribution arrangements exist (or the cost of setting them up is too high) then this could make the segment unprofitable/unviable.

(e) **Measurable**: we must be able to get at the segment in order to establish its characteristics.

(f) **Mutually exclusive**: the segment should not overlap with other segments so that confusion in targeting marketing messages is minimised.

(g) **Homogeneous**: the members of the segment should be sufficiently similar in characteristics to allow suitable messages to be designed.

Consumer markets

In segmenting a consumer market, for example shampoo, we might consider certain factors as the basis of establishing segments.

(a) **Behavioural factors** focusing on usage of the product (eg light, medium, heavy usage), fitness types needing a shower/shampoo etc

(b) **Demographics** - combining age, sex with class, status, religion, occupation

(c) **Family Life Cycle** - aimed at all the family/new babies/thinning hair etc

(d) **Psychographic factors** - AIO analysis (attitudes, interests, opinions), lifestyle

(e) **Geographical factors** - location

(f) **Benefits** - where the messages are aimed at specific wants or needs

Continuing with the shampoo example, we could have separate packaging for men and women, 'sensitive mild' for young children with tender scalps, 'wash'n go' for the fitness types in a hurry, anti-dandruff, shampoos to add 'body' to thinning hair, products with hair tinting, darkening, lightening and so on.

For the higher-income, more socially-conscious individuals, we could offer a higher priced 'studio' name to compete with the Vidal Sassoon range. In contrast, economy ranges could be marketed. Another approach could be to go for the segment who may appreciate taking time and effort to look after themselves and care about their hair, we could follow the 'Pantene' formula-driven approach. Here the appeal would be 'scientific' rather than on 'get it over and done with'.

In contrast, a company selling motor scooters would most likely use age, geography, lifestyle and Family Life Cycle as the key segmentation variables. Once again it is possible to envisage a number of basically similar models being 'packaged' differently to appeal to different segments of the total possible market.

Industrial markets

Here we could segment (say) printing services on the basis of factors such as the following.

(a) **Geography** - concentration of location or distance from the plant

(b) **Type of industry** - we could target label users, magazine publishers etc

(c) **Expenditure** - we may wish to target expensive, high priced 'Rolls Royce' services

(d) **Number of employees** - the size of organisations could be used as the basis for segments

(e) **Turnover** - the level of turnover could be significant and useful

(f) **Usage rates** - we may wish to go for high, low or medium levels of usage, orders and re-orders

(g) **DMU** - we may wish to separate segments for users (product specifications, quality) and deciders (financial data)

An example of industrial segmentation could be if we were to segment on company size. Small firms, for instance, could be offered short-run work such as stationery items, whereas if we were targeting larger firms we could aim to produce their in-house publications, art work, typesetting, editing - the full service, in fact.

The **type** of industry might also be a factor: a small local firm would not expect to pay for overnight turnaround (they probably could not afford to). Targeting a larger company, with greater volume, might be more profitable in the long term, even allowing for bulk discount.

While exclusivity was a characteristic factor for the design of segments, this sometimes causes confusion, as the notion may have to exist in multi-dimensional space. A simple analogy might be that of a series of sieves. We could aim our shampoo at:

Men	sieve 1
Middle aged	sieve 2
Greying	sieve 3
Thinning	sieve 4

Thus the segment is refined successively, allowing ever more specific messages to be designed and delivered.

30 SEGMENTATION SYSTEM

To:	Mr A Gerry
	Marketing Director
	The Gerry Building Company
From:	I.M. Keen, Marketing Consultant
Date:	December 8 2000

Segmentation

Definition

A major problem of mass marketing is the question of whether universal messages and products are appropriate. To make things more manageable it helps to segment the market. This involves the breakdown of the total, broad and varied market into groups. The aim of the process is to identify groups whose constituent members have characteristics in common and in this way messages and products can be tailored specifically to address the needs and wants of the group. Successful segmentation also produces groups (segments) which are significantly different from one another in their requirements. In practical terms it also needs segments which are:

(a) Accessible.
(b) Stable.
(c) Large enough to make marketing worthwhile and profitable.
(d) Different, ideally, from other segments of the population.

Benefits of market segmentation

In addition to the original idea of targeting marketing messages, it is also possible to look at segmentation as a process by which we could develop modified products (or even design new products/services) to fit that segment.

It also allows:

(a) Better marketing planning.
(b) Efficient budget allocation.
(c) Clear focus for marketing efforts.
(d) More discriminating attacks on specialised segments.

Segments will also be the focus of marketing research activity: sometimes we may research to define the needs, wants and aspirations of the segment but in other cases we may well be investigating in order to identify the segment in the first place.

Approaches to segmentation

It is possible to identify five broad approaches to the segmentation problem.

(a) **Geographic.** Here the market is broken down geographically, so it may prove useful to look at areas of a country or (in more detail) postcodes.

(b) **Demographic.** In this case we divide the market by demographic characteristics such as gender and age. There are some well-known combinations of these first two categories (not surprisingly called geo-demographic segmentation) such as the ACORN classification of residential neighbourhoods.

(c) **Class and status.** This is a well-known method for breaking down a large collection of people and is useful if we find a class (or status grouping) which is suitably homogeneous for our purposes. This form of segmentation is useful as it has some built-in assumptions that income and expenditure levels correspond to social class.

(d) **Life stage.** This utilises the Family Life Cycle concept and emphasises that people go through comparable stages in their lives which influence both the types of product they are interested in, and the level of disposable income. It also encompasses families as decision and consuming units in addition to the individuals making up the family.

(e) **Lifestyle or AIO.** This splits the market up by way of values, activities, interests and opinions. As a segmentation approach it has the benefit of focusing directly on what people value and what they spend their cash on (that is, their lifestyle).

Application to the housing market

An evaluation of these systems in the context of the construction industry would lead to the conclusion that geographic segmentation has a useful role as the product (housing) is particularly geographically specific.

Similarly, age and some other demographic factors could be of potential interest and use (homes for the elderly, for students or for singles could be a possibility).

Geo-demographic approaches such as ACORN would be very relevant if you are seeking to develop sites which are already residential - either in making the new properties 'fit in', or in establishing a 'new' image for an old area.

The Family Life Cycle looks to be particularly potent as a device for such a market and is already well established. Starter homes, retirement bungalows, student accommodation and homes for families with small children would all be relevant examples.

The AIO analysis looked to be less relevant for housing as this is in some ways less linked to activities and interests unless we are thinking of specialised theme developments (eg built around a lake with sailing facilities close by). On the other hand, it could be argued that the 'yuppie' lifestyle defined certain types of housing quite effectively.

Conclusion

Residential accommodation would seem to be a market ideally suited to the segmentation approach. From the forgoing summaries it is evident that more than one type of segmentation system can, and should, be applied. None of the systems outlined above are mutually exclusive and they can be used 'in series' either to identify products for an existing segment or to target a segment for an existing product.

As an example it could be possible to identify specific product designs which would suit middle-class professional couples in their early 30's, with small children, in a 'desirable' location. Or alternatively we could conduct market research to establish possible new segments for the 'Buckingham' range of houses you already build.

I suggest that there is a useful project to be conducted to develop a 'mix and match' system which will usefully define the options and needs for your company.

I will be happy to meet you with a view to establishing the parameters for such an assignment.

31   THE DEATH OF SEGMENTATION

> **Tutorial note**. Segmentation is a highly-examinable topic. You should be well prepared to deal with questions on this subject area.

To: L. Ecturer
From: S. Tudent
Date: December 6 2000
Subject: The death of segmentation

I was really interested to read the draft of your chapter on segmentation, with its challenging title and lively argument about the future. I would like to put forward some ideas of my own which might continue the debate still further.

(a) **Reasons for segmentation.** The basic idea underlying the practice of market segmentation is to split a large and extremely diverse market into smaller sub-sets which have individual members who have a greater degree of homogeneity (characteristics which are similar). Once we have defined the needs, wants and other characteristics of the sub-groups we are in a position to do a number of things. The first and most obvious one is to communicate with the sub-groups; but perhaps even more importantly we can establish precisely what their marketing (product or service) needs are. Products and services can then be modified (or even developed) to satisfy a particular segment of the whole market. In simple managerial terms it allows us to schedule priorities in the allocation of marketing resources.

(b) **Characteristics of segments.** To be useful, segments need to be accessible, stable and large enough to support the relevant marketing effort.

(c) **Segmentation systems.** There are numerous approaches to segmenting markets.

   (i)   Geographical.
   (ii)   Social class and status.
   (iii)   Gender and age (demographics).
   (iv)   Family life cycle (FLC).
   (v)   Lifestyle.

   All of these systems allow complex, large markets to be broken down into more manageable units. While each may be of value in different situations (geographical might be significant for clothing markets, FLC for childrens' prams and so on), they all have their limitations and dangers.

(d) **Dangers of segmentation.** It is dangerous to assume that everyone in the sub-set has the same characteristics. An example might arise when considering gender. Segmentation is useful in distinguishing products that are of relevance to women, but may over-simplify the situation if it leads to the conclusion that all women are interested in the same things. Thus we may need more than one segmentation system if we are to identify those women who need to be targeted for particular products. For example, it would be of little help to define the market as being simply female if we are aiming to market products such as the contraceptive pill or 'haute couture' designer label clothes.

(e) **Changing aspirations of consumers.** As our society develops, the expectations of customers are rising. The development in some markets of an approach known as **'mass customisation'** allows the customer to define exactly what it is they, as an individual, want, and the organisation will provide a 'customised' (although probably made from standardised sub-units) product for that specific individual. Examples include Nissan's plans to implement a system where the customer 'designs' the car they require and the company then builds it; Compaq computers and Raleigh bicycles have similar schemes; and Levi jeans have launched a scheme whereby they hold the detailed fitting requirements for individual customers and will make a pair of jeans tailored to those specifications whenever the customer requires replacements. Clearly there are some limitations to such approaches as it implies that customer know exactly what they want and have the technical knowledge to specify those requirements. The Levi example also appears to suffer from an assumption that customers' measurements remain unchanged!

Conclusion

When we look at the examples given in the previous paragraph, it might seem that this proves your case that 'segmentation is dead'. But I would argue that we might then fall into the trap of 'proving' a hypothesis from a small number of unrepresentative examples, however. The limitations to the approach identified above imply that mass customisation would not be suitable for all markets. Even in the Raleigh bicycles case, the scheme only covers a small section of the total bicycle market, only being applicable for those customers who are enthusiasts and are prepared to spend additional money to obtain a unique machine to their own, individual specification. The remainder of the market is segmented using more traditional systems. Indeed, it could be argued that people who are attracted to defining their own cars or having Levi hold their measurements on file represent a segment in their own right, being separate from the vast majority of car or jeans buyers!

Nevertheless, if present trends continue, we may well move further down the mass customisation road. In practice I suspect that the crucial point is that traditional segmentation methods are proving inadequate to cope with the growing demands of customers. What we need, rather than the abandonment of segmentation, is **better** segmentation. What may well be required is more accurate, detailed systems such as those offered by the major supermarkets, whereby actual purchasing patterns are used to define groups (and individuals).

I wonder if you might therefore consider retitling the chapter 'Segmentation is dead - long live segmentation'!

32 ATTITUDES AND BEHAVIOUR

> **Tutorial note.** Perhaps the greatest danger in this question is to see the word 'attitudes' and write all you know about the subject! So after an introduction in which you show you know the basics, keep the focus firmly on the relationship between attitudes and behaviour.

Introduction

Behaviour is what people actually do while attitudes are 'an overall evaluation that enables one to respond in a consistently favourable or unfavourable manner with respect to a given object or alternative' (Engel, Blackwell & Miniard).

Attitudes

Attitudes relate to persons, objects or behaviours that are part of the individual's perceptual world. They represent our basic orientation towards a given stimulus and, as such, form an important part of the way in which people perceive and react to their environments. Attitudes influence, and are influenced by, our goals, perceptions and motivation.

Attitudes are learned and are relatively enduring. They do change, but usually only slowly. They imply evaluation and feeling.

Attitudes have three components.

(a) **Affectivity**: emotional element may be positive or negative.

(b) **Cognition**: knowledge element concerning belief/disbelief.

(c) **Conation**: predisposition or behaviour tendency element.

An attitude must have all three components and it is this fact that distinguishes it from an opinion or belief, which have no affective or feeling component.

Some define an attitude by the expression

$$\textbf{Attitude} = \textbf{Belief} \times \textbf{Value}$$

Attitudes may be:

(a) Positive or negative.

(b) Strong or weak.

(c) Simple or complex.

Attitudes and behaviour

Marketing specialists are interested in people's behaviour because, at an intuitive level, the importance of attitudes in marketing seems obvious: if we believe that a product has certain desirable characteristics, it seems probable that we will like the product and should the appropriate situation arise, we would purchase the product.

All things being equal, people generally behave in a manner consistent with their attitudes and intentions. Certainly, in everyday life we assume that there is a positive relationship between attitudes and behaviour. We attempt to 'change people's minds' about issues we care about, on the assumption that this will result in the behaviour we desire. Gellerman has described attitudes as 'leading variables' to behaviour (ie attitude change predates and

$$\text{Attitude} \longrightarrow \text{Behaviour}$$

On the other hand, particular behaviour often leads to outcomes, which form our attitudes. This suggests that we may also have a relationship such as:

$$\text{Behaviour} \longrightarrow \text{Attitude}$$

The combination is usually represented by the symbol:

$$\text{Attitude} \longleftrightarrow \text{Behaviour}$$

This emphasises that our attitudes may influence our behaviour, but our behaviour may also, in turn, affect our attitudes, either by changing them or by confirming them.

Scenario 1

The initial relationship suggests that attitudes lead to behaviour. Suppose an individual has a positive attitude to the pop group 'The Chemical Brothers'. This may lead her to buy CDs, magazines featuring the group and ancillary merchandise.

Scenario 2

It has already suggested that the relationship may be the other way round - attitudes may be influenced by behaviour. You might get 'dragged along' to see a film that you have a negative attitude towards because of group (or partner) pressure, and find that you actually enjoy it and so your attitude to the film changes.

Scenario 3

There may be no link between some attitudes and behaviour. A person might have a positive attitude towards Ferrari motor cars but a lack of cash means that there is no chance of that person purchasing one.

Scenario 4

The link may exist as described in scenario 1 but the relationship may be weaker than suggested there. There may be a positive attitude towards a product relating to the group but other factors, such as the following, play their part.

(a)   Unforeseen environmental events or situations.
(b)   Lack of control over key factors in the decision-making process.
(c)   Change of mind (or attitude) with time elapsing.
(d)   New information.
(e)   Do not need the object.
(f)   Give in to partner or peer group to keep the peace.

Conclusion

While attitudes are significant, they may not hold the whole story of behaviour. Consider environmental issues. It is possible that many individuals hold positive attitudes about pollution but this does not translate into the purchase of biodegradable washing powders, washing-up liquids, organic fruit and vegetables - or becoming a 'mole' as a protest against the latest by-pass. Key distortions would appear to be areas such as economics, where financial necessity may determine many of our decisions, and peer group pressure to conform to the socially-accepted norms of our social groups.

33   ATTITUDES AND PURCHASES

> **Tutorial note.** Part (a) is quite straightforward 'book' material - but spend a little time in thinking through and planning your response to part (b).

It would be very convenient if attitudes always predicted behaviour, however, experience leads us to the conclusion that a more realistic model might be:

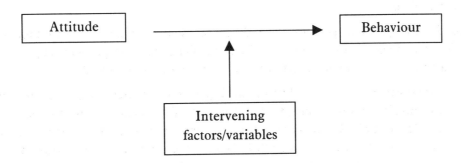

An alternative version might be the idea that 'life gets in the way of what we would wish'.

(a)   **Favourable attitudes may not lead to significant purchases because although we like the product**

   (i)   We may not be able to afford it.

   (ii)   Unforeseen events may intervene, such as a car breaking down which prevents us doing the shopping at the location intended.

   (iii) We may like the product but it is a joint purchase and we 'give in' to our partner's wishes.

   (iv)   Factors outside of our control - the weather may wash out our planned and desired picnic.

   (v)   We may not hold the attitude very strongly - ie we may not care that much.

(vi) An attitude may be generalised rather than specific (I like white wine in general - but not Lambrusco).

(vii) We change our minds over a period of time.

(viii) The original measurement of our attitude may have been inadequate or wrong.

Unfavourable attitudes may generate purchase decisions because, although we dislike the product

(i) It may be the only thing available eg a classic 'distress' purchase such as buying petrol at motorway services.

(ii) As above, we might dislike a product, but our partner in the decision making process is strongly in favour and we acquiesce to keep the peace.

(iii) Again, we may not care that much - we may not hold the attitude that strongly.

(iv) We may be addicted to a product which we hold a negative attitude about - an example might be people who fail to give up smoking, drinking, eating or drugs even though they want to.

(b) **How do we avoid the dangers of false conclusions in marketing research?**

In many ways this could be considered the 'million dollar question' as the problems outlined in section (a) have misled many an organisation introducing a new product. It may be useful, firstly, to note that attitudes are generally accepted to have three dimensions:

(i) Cognitive - concerned with knowledge and beliefs.
(ii) Affective - concerned with feelings and emotions.
(iii) Conative - concerned with behaviour.

In attitude measurement we have developed measures, such as Likert scales and Semantic differential, which are more suited to the first two elements than the behavioural one.

Secondly, the question specifies 'a brand new product'. In this instance we may have a particular and significant problem if the respondents have no previous experience of comparable products/services. Here the issue centres on these issues.

(i) 'Hypothetical answers to hypothetical questions' - which are particularly prone to a number of distortions. One is that we might express favour of something 'in an ideal world' - the current government plans to reduce car usage in town might be an example - we are nearly all in favour of less road congestion and, in theory, we say we would want less cars on the roads, but when it is a rainy morning, and you are late for work, it is all too tempting to get in the car.

(ii) The 'politically correct answer' to market research questions. Here an example might be organic vegetables - we respond to questions by saying that we are in favour, but are then seduced by the vast supermarket display which are also cheaper than the more limited display of less attractive product in the organic section.

To combat these problems, the market researcher can take these steps.

(a) Make allowances for such optimism when evaluating and interpreting research data.

(b) Use more trials of the product. This allows the researcher to follow up on individuals' **actual** experience of the product/service and, it is to be hoped, obtain a much more realistic response and prediction of purchasing behaviour.

(c) Focus on 'innovators' and 'early adopters'. If we are considering a brand new product then our knowledge of the adoption process could be useful. By concentrating on these specific sub-sets of the market, we would gain a more relevant insight into the response of the **initially** crucial groups, thus the innovators and early adopters to purchase, we are in with a good chance of allowing imitation and the adoption process to work to our advantage and set us off on the trail of effectively competing in the whole market.

Needless to say, these options are not exclusive and one could easily conceive of a research project that would utilise all three of the suggested solutions.

34 REASONS AND MOTIVES

There are many forms of consumer behaviour research that tell the marketer what consumers do, where and when. However, marketers are understandably also interested in why people buy and consume certain products in certain ways. In the words of Charles Handy: 'If we could understand, and could then predict, the ways in which individuals were motivated, we could influence them by changing the components of that motivation process.'

Difficulties of motivation research

The main problems of finding out the reasons and motives behind consumer decisions are as follows:

(a) Motives are only 'hypothetical constructs': they can be inferred from behaviour, but not directly observed or measured. Inferences and assumptions on the part of researchers may simply not be accurate - and are unlikely to be totally objective.

(b) If researchers ask the consumers themselves what the reasons or motives for their behaviour are, there are further problems for these reasons.

   (i)   Consumers may not be aware of all their feelings, attitudes and motives with regard to a product or act of purchase.

   (ii) Even if they are aware, they may falsify their responses - perhaps in an attempt to create a good impression or because of suspicion of the researchers' questions.

   (iii) They may not be able to articulate the complex calculations and impulses that motivate behaviour.

   (iv) They may be inhibited because of self-consciousness at being questioned and analysed.

(c) It is difficult to find a measurement technique that is both valid and reliable.

Overcoming these difficulties

Researchers overcome the problem of single-technique reliability by commonly using a combination of research methods.

In order to tackle the problem that motives may not be consciously recognised, nor easily or accurately revealed, by consumers, researchers attempt to uncover subconscious processes, by not approaching the question of purchase motivation directly. The two main techniques used are as follows.

(a) The 'depth interview' is a technique drawn from clinical psychology. It is generally informal, and relies on the encouragement of the subject(s) to talk freely about the relevant subject (say, aspects of a buying situation), rather than on a question-and-answer agenda. The participants are not necessarily told what the specific topic under research is: they are thus less likely to 'second guess' the interviewer. The topics and

BPP
PUBLISHING

images that come up in discussion and the areas that get most emphasis offer the interviewer information about the participants' perceptions of the subject, as well as about the subject itself.

(b) Group interviews (sometimes also called 'focus groups') typically consist of eight to ten participants. They allow a larger sampling of opinions to be gathered with less time and cost, and are more 'realistic' in allowing social factors to influence individuals' perceptions. Ideas can be exchanged and adjusted. The influence of dominant individuals and the desire to conform to the prevailing group attitudes can also be observed. Interviewers should, however, control this tendency where possible, or they will never be sure whether 'the group' held an opinion or merely stayed quiet - conforming or not- while a dominant individual stated his view.

(c) Projective techniques were also borrowed from clinical psychology, designed to reflect the motives of individuals despite their attempts at rationalisation or concealment. Subjects are presented with ambiguous stimuli (uncaptioned cartoons, incomplete sentences, random marks) and asked to complete, describe or explain them: the subjects' inner feelings influence the way they perceive and interpret the stimuli.

Examples of projective techniques

(i) **Rorschach Inkblot Test** Subjects are shown inkblots and asked to describe what they see, in order to expose dominant imagery and preoccupations.

(ii) **Word association**. Subjects are presented with a series of words or phrases and asked to respond quickly with the first word that comes to mind after each 'cue'. Among neutral 'cues' will be some that are related to aspects of the product category or brand being researched: association will indicate how the product or brand is perceived. Marketers may also use this technique to try out brand names, to see which potential words or phrases are best understood and perceived in the most desirable way.

(iii) **The Thematic Apperception Test**. Subjects are asked to interpret (tell a story about, or add captions or 'thought bubbles' to) one or more pictures or cartoons relating in some aspect to the topic being researched: they tend to identify with one of the characters depicted, or to identify themes and images in the situation that reflect their own feelings.

Conclusion

Despite the problems associated with motivation research, and the use of projective techniques in particular, subconscious motivation is still believed to be vitally important in consumer choice, and qualitative techniques can give marketers a deeper insight into those areas than conventional, quantitative marketing research.

35   MOTIVATIONAL THEORIES

> **Tutorial note.** Full marks to the examiner for asking this question in the first place. People tend to trot out the 'standard' motivation theory with very little thought about its real usefulness. You may have reached different conclusions to those in our answer.

Introduction

The three theories of motivation that I have chosen to review are Maslow's Hierarchy of Needs, Vroom's Expectancy Theory, and Herzberg's Two-Factor Theory.

The Theories

(a) **Maslow's Hierarchy of Needs**

This theory groups needs into broad categories, arranges them into a hierarchy of prepotency, and theorises on their relationships. The notion of prepotency implies 'overriding force' and proposes that some groups of needs will take precedence over others when the individual is faced with choices as to which needs to satisfy. The hierarchy is commonly displayed as a pyramid or triangle:

SELF ACTUALISATION
the need to realise one's potential by using all of one's talents.

ESTEEM
the need for self-respect and self-confidence. Respect, recognition and appreciation of others.

COMPANIONSHIP
the need for group membership. Friendship, affection and acceptance of one's peers

SECURITY
the need to have a degree of safety in one's life, freedom from bodily harm or threat. This may also extend to safety of prized elements of lifestyle.

PHYSIOLOGICAL
basic to everyone are the needs for food, water, shelter, rest and sex. Without fulfilment of these needs most persons are not motivated by higher needs.

Maslow's hypothesis is that a satisfied need is no longer a motivator and that the hierarchy operates such that a person's behaviour will tend to be dominated by trying to satisfy the lowest unsatisfied need. Thus physiological needs will tend to take precedence over security, companionship or esteem needs. One particular class of needs must reach a sufficient level of satisfaction before the next needs level becomes operational. The emphasis is on sufficiency - each successive level must be relatively satisfied before the next level of need becomes more important in motivating behaviour.

Another view of the prepotency approach is that an individual is continually responding to the 'lowest' unsatisfied need. In reality the different categories of needs may operate on very different timescales. Food needs could be defined in terms of calories/day whilst self-actualisation may be a lifetime target measured in years. This has given rise to the observation that for many people life is a struggle to achieve higher level satisfactions against the 'obstacles' of lower level needs.

(b) **Vroom's Expectancy theory**

This approach assumes that individuals make rational decisions based on the importance of the outcome to them and their perception of the likelihood of that outcome arising from an action. Vroom puts forward four premises:

(i) People have preferences (valences) for various outcomes or incentives that are available to them.

(ii) People hold expectations about the probability that an action or effort on their part will lead to the intended outcome or objective.

(iii) People understand that certain behaviours will be followed by desirable outcomes or incentive rewards, eg a pay rise or increased status.

(iv) The action a person chooses to take is determined by the expectancies and preferences (valences) that the person has at the time. The relationship is commonly presented as follows.

$$F = E \times V$$

Where
F = motivation to behave
E = expectation that the behaviour will be followed by a particular outcome (subjective probability)
V = valence of the outcome

The hypothesis is that we will behave in the way which we believe will give the most desired outcome overall.

(c) **Herzberg's two-factor theory**

This draws a distinction between:

(i) 'satisfaction' in the sense of a positive, conscious state of elation; and
(ii) 'satisfaction' as a neutral state reflecting an absence of negative sensations.

Herzberg classified the positive satisfiers as 'motivators' while the neutral version (or potential dissatisfiers) he refers to as 'maintenance' or 'hygiene' factors.

His studies suggested the following:

Hygiene/maintenance factors	Motivators
Company policy & administration	Achievement
Supervision	Recognition
Salary	Work itself
Interpersonal relations	Responsibility
Physical working conditions	Advancement

The theory suggest that the presence of dissatisfiers causes low work performance, so the maintenance 'hygiene factors must be put right. However, this does not lead to motivation, only to the 'no dissatisfaction' type of 'satisfaction'. Motivation (and hence high work performance) is generated by the motivators.

Review of theories and applications to marketing

Maslow's theory is perhaps the most all-embracing and influential theory in common currency. It provides a useful device for the description and explanation of behaviour - but it is significantly weaker at prediction. Many discussions of its application rapidly become arguments on semantics with more energy spent on defining words that on validating the model. This seems to reflect the importance (and variety) of individual perceptions of what constitutes the needs in each broad category.

There are other problems with the theory.

(i) There is a lack of empirical evidence to support it.

(ii) Self-actualisation and esteem needs are likely to be a function of each individual's self-perception. This in turn may be socially conditioned. Thus we may question whether we are describing an innate need or something which may be defined by family, gender, culture and class.

The theory allows us to associate certain products with appropriate levels of the hierarchy and so segment the market into large target populations. It also offers the marketer the opportunity to offer the product as a solution to a problem or the satisfier of a need.

Vroom's approach to motivation appears to be potentially useful to the marketers as it can define strategies for us.

- We aim to increase the perceived value of our product
- We aim to raise the expectancy of satisfaction
- We do both

Marketers must, of course, take great care not to raise consumers' expectations of a product beyond the level that it can satisfy. A very quick way to achieve a poor reputation is to promise things you cannot deliver.

Herzberg's approach can be criticised on a number of grounds, not least that it was based on relatively small sample of engineers and accountants in Pittsburgh, but it has had wide acceptance in the organisational setting. However, it is very much work centred and the potential applications to marketing seem very limited.

36 PSYCHOANALYTICAL THEORY

Freud's psychoanalytic theory stresses the unconscious nature of personality as a result of childhood conflicts. These conflicts are derived from three components of personality, the id, the ego and the superego. The id controls the individual's most basic needs and urges such as hunger, sex and self-preservation. The id is the source of all innate forces that drive behaviour. It operates on one principle – directing behaviour to achieve pleasure and avoid pain. Product categories affected by the id would include basic food and clothing as well as pharmaceutical products such as pain killers. Fragrances would also come into this category as the vast majority imply that the wearer will be more attractive and successful in their relationships as a direct result of wearing their fragrance. Products that have the potential to be addictive such as alcohol and tobacco would also be applicable. Computer games allow players to display emotions that would not be appropriate in normal life eg high speed competitive driving or armed combat.

The ego is the individual's self-concept and is the manifestation of objective reality, as it develops in interaction with the external world. The ego is the manager of the id. It seeks to attain the goals of the id in a socially acceptable manner. For example, rather than manifest a basic need to be aggressive in anti-social ways, an individual may partially satisfy this need by buying a powerful car. Designer clothing and other status related products would also fall into this category.

The superego does not manage the id but restrains it by punishing unacceptable behaviour through the creation of guilt. Like the id, it operates in the unconscious and often represses behaviour that would otherwise occur based on the id. The superego represents the ideal rather than the real. It motivates consumers to act in a normal way. Many products play on the guilt emotion. These include slimming aids, insurance policies and children's products.

37 DMU

MEMORANDUM

To: I. Know, Marketing Director
From: T. Rainset, Marketing Consultant
Date: December 6 2000
Subject: Marketing toys - some ideas

As part of our review of marketing strategy I would like to put forward some ideas for discussion at our next planning meeting.

(a) **Customers and users**

Authors such as Johns (1994) have drawn a distinction between customers and users.

'Customers' are people who use our services and pay for them. 'Users' are individuals who are affected by or who affect the product that we supply. Users often use the product but do not pay for it.

Although a significant amount of business comes from selling smaller, cheaper, 'pocket-money' toys, the distinction between customers and users is most obvious in relation to our more expensive products. Children do not buy the toys in this category - parents, relatives and friends of the family do. It may therefore be valuable to focus our attention on the interests, motivations and emotional values attached to toys by such groups.

When purchasing our products, these customers could be attempting to purchase love or peace and quiet!

(i) Granny buying a teddy bear for a grandchild wants the child to fall in love with the bear and to express delight and love in return. This is likely to be a major motivation for many 'givers'.

(ii) Alternatively a child may have pestered his parent unmercifully for, let's say, a skateboard. The parent, driven to distraction, finally gives in. In this case the payoff is peace and an absence of demands.

(iii) Continuing with the child/adult situation, we are likely to find that some presents are purchased by customers who never had one as a child and can now fulfil the dream. The train set for the child which is played with by the father and the other who buys the child ballet lessons or a pony as a vicarious fulfilment of her own dream are examples.

In such cases we need to be concerned with satisfying the user (the child) - but only as a means of satisfying the real, paying customer.

(b) **Segmentation**

This idea of targeting the marketing message at the 'right' person leads into another idea which may help develop the framework for analysing our marketing strategy. The aim of segmenting a market is to identify groups whose constituent members have characteristics in common, so that messages and products can be tailored specifically to address the needs and wants of the group. Successful segmentation produces groups (segments) which are significantly different from one another in their requirements but we also need to identify segments which are accessible, stable, and which are large enough to make marketing worthwhile and profitable.

Traditionally there are four broad systems of segmentation.

(i) **Demographically** gender, geography, culture and age.

(ii) **Life stage** particularly well utilised in marketing is the Family Life Cycle.

(iii) **Lifestyle** (sometimes called psychographics): looks at the personalities, values, interests and activities of the target market, and also includes the usage/satisfactions sought.

In the toy market several of these systems would seem to be relevant.

(i) **Demographic segmentation** is relevant when a toy is targeted at specific age groups and (at the risk of appearing politically incorrect) when different toys are targeted at girls and boys. The geographical segmentation is less relevant generally, but culture could be an important tool in opening up new markets.

(ii) **Life stage segmentation** is utilised overtly by organisations such as 'Mothercare', parents being a specific market segment (Full Nests etc). This system would clearly help us, although if we are aiming at a wider audience of grannies, uncles and so on, the traditional FLC is rather less useful.

(iii) **Class and status segmentation** could be important for some products. Pacifiers/dummies may be seen as unsuitable by those aspiring to higher social standing, while backgammon may be seen by some as a 'snobby' game.

(iv) **Lifestyle** could be the most significant system for us as it could help to identify and target those who seek 'educational' toys (note the use of 'Early Learning Centre' as a brand name appealing direct to such people) in contrast to those who seek 'fun' toys (from Toys 'R'Us?).

It would seem possible that several of these could be used immediately to help us in developing our marketing strategy.

(c) **Decision Making Units**

Finally, we need to compare the customer/user with the roles in the Decision Making Unit (DMU) favoured in organisational buying. Children are likely to be the key Influencers, given the emotional influence that a child can wield over the significant Adults (our customers).

In the context of the toy industry, the distinction between customer and user seems clear. The child will still remain a significant target for marketing messages as the key influencer (via 'pesterpower') in the social DMU, however, so advertising can continue to be directed at children. The major insight of the analysis, however, is the need to centre attention on the paying customer. Parents are likely to fulfil 'gatekeeper', 'preparer', 'financier', 'decider' and 'buyer' roles for many of our more expensive toys. It may therefore be necessary to undertake market research to explore the motivation and emotional values adults attach to the process of giving presents to children. This insight could give us a significant competitive edge over the organisation that thinks that its customer is the child.

38 TYPES OF GROUP

Human beings are social animals and membership of a variety of groups is a standard experience for almost everybody. Groups are a significant **source of emotional satisfaction** and also of **social class and status**. Group membership involves social interaction and a degree of give-and-take; **acceptance by the group** is the motivation of the individual and the price of membership is conformity to the group norms. This conforming is the element which is of interest to marketers as it illustrates how influential groups can be in terms of individual behaviour. If groups can influence behaviour it may be possible, through studying their processes, to understand and possibly influence buying behaviour. Additionally groups may be a useful way of segmenting a particular market.

(a) Ascribed **groups** which are groups to which a person automatically belongs - examples include the family, male/female and so on.

(b) Acquired **groups,** on the other hand are those of which a person has sought membership, for example the Chartered Institute of Marketing.

These are relevant as ascribed groups may, in the case of the family, be powerful decision making and purchasing groups. Ascribed groups such as gender will segment the market effectively in terms of sex-specific products while colour of skin could make a particularly potent market segment for some products such as a non-pink version of 'Elastoplast'. The acquired groups are also significant as the act of acquisition implies a degree of motivation -

that is, 'I want to join the golf club'. Here the marketing of the symbols of membership may be the main opportunity.

A second distinction may be made between:

(a) Primary **groups**, which are usually small with close emotional contact and face-to-face communication - for example family, friendship groups.

(b) Secondary **groups**, which are more impersonal in terms of communication and are commonly larger. Examples are societies, colleges, and organisations.

The relevance of these lies in the power of the emotional influence of the primary group and the larger size (and hence greater purchasing power) of the secondary group which is commonly more concerned with organisational buying. It is interesting that much effort is expended in many secondary groups (such as organisations) to develop the emotional commitment found in primary groups.

A further distinction must be made between:

(a) **Formal groups**, which have a clearly defined purpose or goal with defined roles - for example an **Understanding Customers** class with teacher/student roles.

(b) **Informal groups**, which usually exist to satisfy the social needs of the members. Roles still exist but are rarely allocated formally. Examples would include groups of friends which may exist quite comfortably **within** a more formal grouping.

Again, the significance of the formal group lies in its size, formality, its capacity to impose on members ('you will need to buy the course book') and its potential as a purchasing unit in its own right. The informal groups may be centred on common interests which could offer huge marketing opportunities in providing materials, equipment or services for those interests. Perhaps the most obvious would be the informal group of friends who enjoy shopping together as a social activity (whether shopping entails touring departmental stores, drinking, going to the cinema or supporting a football team).

Membership groups are those groups to which an individual **belongs** whether they are formal or informal, whereas **aspirational groups** are those groups to which the individual does not belong to but to which the person wishes to belong.

Membership groups are significant by definition (everything discussed above applies as the individual is a member of the particular group) while aspirational groups are important as they represent an unsatisfied need which offers clear and potent marketing opportunities as people seek to achieve their desires or, at least, to acquire the trappings, symbols and artefacts of membership of the aspirational group.

It may be worth mentioning **dissociative groups** which are those the individual wishes not to be associated with (usually because of values and behaviour) - again there may be a chance of marketing activity in reinforcing the difference from the dissociative groups.

One aspect which may need to be clarified is the idea that specific groups can fall into more than one category - for instance your family group may well be both ascribed and primary as well as being a membership group which is both formal and possesses many characteristics of an informal group.

39   BUYER BEHAVIOUR

Introduction

The presentation will focus on the product/service characteristics which might define the suitability for global marketing or national marketing or global market but adapted to local conditions.

Global marketing is the situation where a product is sold in identical form throughout the world. It normally involves similar marketing and promotion and may be viewed as a 'universal' product.

National marketing is used to describe the situation where the product/service is more suited to localised marketing and is part of a specific culture.

Global marketing adapted to local conditions is the half-way house - the global product and organisation exists, but the product/service is modified to fit the local conditions.

Main points for presentation

(a)   The issues which will form the basis of any decision will centre on the compatibility of the product/service being marketed to any national or local culture. We might call such criteria the **'cultural fit'** of the product.

(b)   It is clear that key elements of a **culture** (language, religious beliefs, eating patterns, gender roles and so on) will be the sensitive factors in the decision.

(c)   **Global** marketing will be most relevant in a situation where the **product is not culturally sensitive.** Time is one relatively universal concept and so watches might fall into such a category. Electronic products generally fall into a similar category and have the advantage of appealing to younger generations who may carry less cultural baggage and identify more with the 'universal American TV culture'. There is also the possibility that our product will be directed at a specific 'micro-culture'. Here an example might be the market for designer clothes and accessories, here the micro-culture (or market) at which such expensive items are aimed have a 'universal' commonality which crosses national barriers (that is, they are the members of the rich 'jet set').

(d)   National or local marketing will be more appropriate where a product is culturally sensitive. Here the issues of language, eating and social roles may be significant with the usual examples of not selling pork products in the Jewish/Moslem cultures and are relevant. Some products are highly language sensitive - greetings cards or audio tapes would be examples - and these are really only applicable in the 'host' culture. Inevitably it would be possible to 'de-sensitise' the product by marketing greeting cards which had no printed message, or audio tapes which were sold as opportunities to learn a language.

(e)   The global/adapted option applies where products operate effectively on a world-wide basis, but which are 'tweaked' to suit the demands of a particular market. Examples here would include motor cars which are offered with right- and left-hand drive according to the country in which they are to be driven. It is also claimed that Nescafe Instant Coffee is produced to slightly different formulae to suit different national tastes.

(f)   Product names can also be problematic when the item crosses cultural barriers. Some of the best know examples include Vauxhall Motors difficulty in marketing a car called a 'Nova' in Spanish speaking countries, as that name translates as 'Does not go'. Toyota's problems with their MR2 sportscar and the marketing of a deodorant called

'Cue' in France have been similarly well documented. Specialist consultants may prove a sound investment when facing name choices for any global product.

Conclusion

If we are seeking to develop criteria by which to make the global/national marketing Choice, we must come up with a list of the crucial elements and 'symptoms' of Culture. A starting point would be likely to include the following.

(a) Language
(b) Eating
(c) Gender roles, but might also include:

   (i)   dress;
   (ii)   relationships;
   (iii) time consciousness;
   (iv)   appearance; and
   (v)   beliefs about work and leisure.

The broader concepts to be considered include:

(a) Religious beliefs.
(b) Education and political systems.
(c) Laws.
(d) Beliefs.
(e) Values.

Running our product against such a checklist could save expensive embarrassment later.

One final issue may well be the need to consider the PEST (political, economic, social and technological) state of the culture to which we may hope to market. If our product demands a technology or infrastructure which is not available the marketing effort will be severely hampered.

40   SECONDARY GROUPS

A group may be defined as two or more people who interact to accomplish either individual or mutual goals. Consumer behaviour is principally concerned with the study of small groups because such groups are more likely to influence consumption behaviour of group members.

(a) **Primary and secondary**

   If a person interacts on a regular basis with other individuals (with members of their family, neighbours, and close colleagues at work), then these individuals can be considered a primary group for that person. On the other hand, if a person interacts only occasionally with others, or does not consider their opinions particularly important, then these others constitute a secondary group for that person. The critical distinction between primary and secondary groups, therefore, are the perceived importance of the groups to the individual and the frequency or consistency with which the individual interacts with them.

(b) **Formal and informal**

   These terms refer to the extent to which the group structure, the members' roles and group's purpose are clearly defined. If a group has a highly defined structure (eg a golf club's membership list), specific roles and authority levels (eg a president, treasurers and secretary) and specific goals (eg to manage funds, arrange social functions), then it would be classified as a formal group. However, if the group is loosely defined, if it consists for example of several individuals who became friends while studying who meet once a month for a drink, then it is considered to be an informal group.

From a consumer behaviour perspective, informal, social or friendship groups are generally more important because their less clearly defined structures provide a more conducive environment for the exchange of information and influence about consumption-related topics.

(c) **Membership and symbolic**

Groups are sometimes classes by membership status. A group to which a person either belongs or would qualify for membership is called a membership group. University alumni associations are membership groups and for marketing practitioners the key group is the Chartered Institute of Marketing.

There are groups in which an individual is not likely to receive membership, despite acting like a member by adopting the group's values, attitudes and behaviour, these are know as symbolic groups. For instance, professional golfers may constitute a symbolic group for an amateur golfer who identifies with certain players by imitating their behaviour whenever possible (eg by purchasing a specific brand of golf clubs or golf balls). The amateur golfer does not, however (and probably never will), qualify for membership as a professional golfer, because he has neither the skills nor the opportunity to compete professionally.

41   BUSINESS BUYING BEHAVIOUR

Marketers have developed different ways of serving household and business customers, in part because of differences in the behaviour of these two customer groups. Business buying typically differs from household buying in several different ways.

(a) **Specialisation of customer roles**

Individual buying requires that the three customer roles - payer, buyer and user - be combined in a single individual, whereas in household buying decisions, these roles may be held by a single person or distributed among various family members. Such role specialisation is even more marked in business buying. Thus, even more than in the household buying, the three roles separate out. An exception to this pattern is a one-person entrepreneur, who makes decisions equivalent to individual decision making.

(b) **Formalisation of the buying process**

Business buying is formalised with respect to policy, procedures and paperwork. Generally, businesses have written policies and rules to guide the solicitation of price quotes, preferential treatment to a certain class of vendor (eg small businesses), and the way the decisions are to be made in the buying firms. They prepare and sign detailed contracts that specify the obligations of each party. This degree is rare in family buying behaviour.

(c) **Accountability for decisions**

Unlike household buying, business buying holds accountable those who are in charge of paying and buying. This results in more formal evaluation of and feedback on these purchase decisions. There are also internal and external audits of the buying process to ensure that value obtained through procurement is maintained and enhanced by the decision makers.

The greater accountability in business arises because ownership is divorced from management, and buying is divorced from usage. Therefore, business buying encourages formal supplier ratings as well as constant feedback and communications to its suppliers.

(d) **Internal capabilities**

More often than households, business customers are capable of producing certain items in-house rather than buying them from others. This capability requires business customers to analyse the economics of the 'make versus buy' options. Even when the decision is to buy, rather than make, the internal capability to make the product gives the buyer power among potential suppliers. Thus, sellers to business customers cannot forget that the customer can become a competitor by self-producing the item rather than buying it.

(e) **Complexity of requirements**

Business customers have both operational and strategic complexity in their buying behaviour. Operationally the number of employees who participate in the buying process, often from several locations, adds complexity. Further complexity results from the need to adhere to government rules and regulations related to reciprocity of buying and selling to one another. Finally, many business-buying decisions involve multiple authority and expertise levels, making the process even more complex.

Additionally, procurement is often a strategic function. It is often the single largest cost centre to a business organisation. This cost centre is responsible for buying both capital goods and materials, so the risks associated with failure are enormous.

42 RESELLERS

A reseller is a licensed business entity that buys someone else's products and services, adds some value for the customer, and sells them to other customers who may themselves be resellers or end users. Typically, a reseller is more involved with creating value for the buyer, whereas a manufacturer of products is more involved with creating value for the user.

The values sought by the customer in their buyer role are service, convenience and personalisation; and a reseller creates these values by creating time and place utilities. Often, however, resellers create values relevant to the user role also, for example, when a jewellery shop sizes a ring, or when a clothing retailer offers alterations. Sometimes the shop name itself adds prestige to the product, thus giving the user social and emotional value. Resellers also tend to add value for the payer role, by offering price value eg bulk buying and by offering credit and finance values.

Since most consumer products tend to be sold through resellers, resellers are very important customers for the manufacturers of consumer durables (such as appliances, cars and consumer electronics) and for consumer non-durables (such as grocery products, pharmaceuticals and household products).

Often, however, resellers create values relevant to the user role also, for example, when a jewellery shop sizes a ring, or when a clothing retailer offers alterations. Sometimes the shop name itself adds prestige to the product, thus giving the user social and emotional value. Resellers also tend to add value for the payer role, by offering price value eg bulk buying and by offering credit and finance values.

Since most consumer products tend to be sold through resellers, resellers are very important customers for the manufacturers of consumer durables (such as appliances, cars and consumer electronics) and for consumer non-durables (such as grocery products, pharmaceuticals and household products).

43   CUSTOMER IS KING

'The customer is king.'

This quote implies that the customer's **wishes are paramount** within the organisation and that their requirements should be put before any others. This certainly supports the customer-centric focus at the heart of marketing, however it assumes that the customer actually knows what they want and has an understanding of how organisations operate. As a customer, I may want high quality, low priced clothing. I may not understand that to obtain this retailers may have to abandon UK based manufacturers and seek supplier in the Far East who may have substantially reduced labour and raw material costs. There is no question that customers need to be listened to as well as communicated with. However, it is the responsibility of organisations to ensure that they are provided with appropriate information to allow them to make informed decisions.

'The customer is always right.'

This saying assumes that in the case of a dispute between a customer and an organisation that the organisation is always at fault. This clearly cannot always be the case. Consumers may be negligent in their use of a product, despite the manufacturer's warnings and organisations cannot be held liable for such behaviour. The situation regarding service encounters is more complex. These tend to arise because the customer has developed certain expectations regarding an organisation eg waiting in a bank queue for less than five minutes, so that when these expectations are not satisfied, they feel they have cause for complaint. It is the responsibility of organisations to ensure that service promises are realistic and deliverable. At the same time it is the responsibility of consumers to make organisations aware of problems so that they may be addressed.

In organisations, some departments or sections are internal customers of other departments' products, or more usually, services. For instance, the computer services division will maintain computer systems for the entire organisation. In such situations it is helpful for those service departments to perceive themselves as providing a service to a customer. Increasingly such services are being outsourced and as such there is no guarantee that those services will always be required. In local government there is now an obligation to consider the option of contracting out.

Such focus may require **a change in organisational culture**, whereby other divisions are viewed as customers rather than colleagues. It also implies are more proactive approach to ensure that customer satisfaction is being achieved and improved. The requirements of internal customers are seldom investigated. The quality implementation process requires that all the supplier/customer relationships within the 'quality chain' should be treated as marketing exercises, and that each customer should be carefully consulted as to their precise requirements from the product or service with which they are to be provided.

In such cases, the needs of **all customers need to be prioritised and balanced** as resources may be constrained – as such it could be said that all customers are princes or princesses, rather than kings and queens. Clear lines of communication need to be maintained to ensure that internal customers have reasonable expectations and the internal service provider has the resources to meet these.

In the past many public-sector service operations were not customer-focused simply because they were monopolies, supplying services like education, housing and refuse collection to 'ratepayers', whether they wanted them or not. Many organisations did not realise that they had customers at all. British Telecommunications (BT) used to call its customers 'subscribers' and kept them diligently at arms-length. Compulsive competitive tendering has been brought into may areas of local government but there are still significant areas that are managed solely by local government. In such cases, the interests of consumers or customers are not placed first in the list of priorities so far as tangible action is concerned. Consumers, customers, clients and council taxpayers may appear first in the corporate rhetoric but that is not permissible as genuine evidence of behaviour. Local authorities need to address the requirements of many customers, all with differing needs and once again, as with internal customers, these needs must be prioritised and managed with finite resources.

44 TUTORIAL QUESTION: THE CASE FOR MARKET RESEARCH

Decisions made by any manager without the benefit of accurate, up-to-date information are bound to be rather hit and miss. Marketing managers especially operate in an ever-changing environment where mistakes are inevitable. An understanding of the political, economic and competitive trends is therefore essential to minimise incorrect and costly decisions.

A certain amount of marketing intelligence will be available to marketing managers in the form of sales force reports, articles in trade journals, company reports and directories such as Kompass and Kelly's. Marketing managers should also have access to good quality internal data relating to order levels and sales, delivery lead times and importance of different customers to the organisation. Desk research will therefore reveal a certain amount of information using secondary sources which can be used to form the basis of good quality marketing decisions and should certainly be a starting point before any primary research is commissioned.

Although this will set the scene, the picture will be incomplete, as it is difficult to get a true feel for the market place, the competition and the customers (existing and potential) without using some primary research.

Market research should allow an organisation to ascertain different types of information.

(a) **Market information**. For example: the total size of the market and own market share; potential for growth; likely threats and opportunities (new products and new markets).

(b) **Competitor information**. Who they are; their relative market shares; their own strengths and weaknesses; their marketing strategy.

(c) **Customer information**. Their opinion of your organisation, the effectiveness of your promotional campaigns and your sales force and those of the competition; their likely future purchases; who the key decision makers are; any logical groupings (segments).

There will of course be situations where it is unrealistic or impractical to commission research.

(a) **Where the cost would outweigh the benefits**. Although better information should help reduce risks, if the cost of obtaining it is higher than the cost of making the wrong decision, it would clearly be unwise to go ahead. A clear set of objectives (in writing) should therefore be established and put into a brief from which a potential supplier of the research can realistically draw up a proposal including full costings.

(b) **Where the potential results would not be useful.** If, for example, a segmentation study were carried out which identified potential groupings of customers which in reality could not be reached or would cost more to reach than selling to existing groupings, it would not be worth commissioning the research.

(c) **Where unfavourable results would be ignored.** Some organisations have been known to use market research to justify their decisions, choosing to ignore the existence of findings, which contradict their own judgement. If this is thought to be the reality, it would be better not to commission the research, as it will not only waste the money of the organisation, but could also adversely affect the goodwill of the consumers/users who participate.

(d) **Where time pressures do not allow primary research to be carried out.**

Apart from the above instances, and assuming that secondary sources have been fully exploited first of all, it is generally felt to be very important and beneficial to commission up-to-date market research to assist in the decision making, both strategic and tactical, of the marketing department.

45   MARKET RESEARCH

(**Assumption:** an undergraduate audience implies relatively high intelligence and verbal skills. As they are Business Studies students they will also be confident with much of the language of business and marketing - therefore I would not attempt to over simplify my talk.)

Introduction

Marketing is defined by the CIM as 'the management process responsible for identifying, anticipating and satisfying consumers' requirements profitably'.

In a dynamic and changing economy there is a clear need for a continuing effort to match the capacities and efforts of the organisation to the needs of customers. A key activity is researching the environment and the market so that these aims of marketing can be fulfilled.

This whole process of collecting the information on consumers in order to answer such questions is commonly called marketing research. It has been defined by the Market Research Society as:

'The collection and analysis of data from a sample of individuals or organisations related to their characteristics, behaviour, attitudes, opinions or possessions. It includes all forms of research such as consumer and industrial surveys, psychological investigations, observational and panel studies...'

What can market research do?

The process of marketing research is used by organisations for a number of purposes.

(a) To identify changes in the existing marketplace
(b) To improve market awareness so as to inform negotiations with suppliers
(c) To build up a bank of information
(d) To solve ad hoc problems
(e) To help in making plans for the future
(f) Monitoring the success of current plans

We could illustrate this by posing some of the questions which a marketing department may be asked to answer.

Some may centre on the **existing market.**

(a)   How big is a given market?

(b)   Is it growing, contracting or stable?

(c)   How profitable is it?

(d)   What differing market segments are apparent?

(e)   How are they different from one another?

(f)   What other products/services are in the market?

(g)   Who are the significant players/competitors?

Others focus on potential markets.

(a)   How can we get ideas for new products/services?

(b)   How do we choose which ideas to develop?

(c)   How do we identify new market segments to target?

Strategic questions may be asked.

(a)   Where do we stand in the market compared to our competitors?

(b)   Should we get out of a given market?

(c)   Should we go into others?

(d)   What marketing strategies are being adopted by our competitors?

Product/service perceptions may need to be established.

(a)   How do consumers see our product/service?

(b)   What product attributes could be enhanced?

(c)   What satisfactions do they provide?

(d)   What is the consumer motivation for purchase?

(e)   How can we choose a 'good' brand name?

(f)   What constitutes a 'good' pack design?

(g)   How can we make our product distinctive?

Pricing issues can be important.

(a)   What is the competition charging?

(b)   What are consumers prepared to pay?

(c)   What do they expect to pay?

(d)   What effect is price likely to have on sales?

Advertising demands answers to **pre-advertising** questions.

(a)   What is the advertising message?

(b)   Who is the advertisement's target?

(c)   What is it going to cost?

(d)   What media are likely to be most effective?

Post-advertising questions might include:

(a)   What messages are being received?

(b)   What level of consumer awareness have we achieved?

(c)   Do the consumers like the advert?

(d)   What associations are consumers making?

(e)   What impact on sales has the campaign achieved?

What can't it do?

Market research is very much a management tool.

(a) It cannot manage for us.

(b) It cannot make decisions for us, although it can be crucial in terms of establishing evidence on which **marketing managers** can make decisions.

(c) It is only strong at dealing with reactions to existing products, services or messages. It cannot reliably gain information about products which do not yet exist and which respondents have had no experience or image of.

(d) In a dynamic marketplace it can only operate with the evidence that has been collected - it cannot predict future product life when it does not know what competitors will come out with and what the marketplace will look like in the future.

Conclusion

Market research is a key activity which must be integral to successful marketing. In one sense its very success has caused some problems. As techniques, both primary and secondary, have developed and become a crucial source of competitive edge, so there has been a tendency to load more onto marketing research than can truly be justified. The fact that it usually has a quantitative element has led to a spurious belief in its accuracy. Similarly it suffers from most of the weaknesses of the behavioural science in terms of prediction and control. It suffers from the potential hazards of the Hawthorne Effect when gathering data (people telling you what they think you want to hear) and it is always susceptible to claims of bias, self-fulfilling prophecies and 'getting the answer that the client/boss wants'.

Nevertheless its advantages are such that no self-respecting professional marketing department would consider operating without it.

46 MARKET RESEARCH METHODOLOGIES

> **Tutorial note.** Note that the examiner will award marks for part (b) of your answer being in report format. You should answer on only one of the four products in part (b). Our answer is only indicative, since we do not know which one you chose.

(a) **Qualitative and quantitative research**

Qualitative research is geared towards gathering qualitative information about, for instance, attitudes and motivation, often in the form of pictures and words and using techniques such as discussion groups. It generates impressions and ideas which can back up the product of quantitative research and can also suggest messages and other elements of the final promotion. Quantitative research is involved with data as numbers, often using questionnaires and surveys. It gives greater reassurance of statistical validity.

Advantages and disadvantages

(i)   Dangers of impressionistic or value-laden interpretation of contributions in qualitative studies

(ii)   Benefits of a two-way information gathering process (qualitative) as opposed to impersonal questionnaires (quantitative)

(iii) Marketing research design process (both)

(iv)   Questionnaire, construction, testing of it, incentives for questionnaire completion

(v)   Interpretation of results, including margins of statistical error (quantitative)

(vi)   Avoidance of wishful thinking (qualitative)

(b)

> **Tutorial note**. Use report format, which means heading up your answer in a way similar to that shown below and dividing your answer up clearly with an introduction, headed sections and clear recommendations.)

To: Marketing Director
From: Mark Research
Date: September 2000
Subject: Marketing research methodology (for one of the four products)

Set out below in outline, are a number of matters that might have been mentioned in your report. You would need to focus on one product and go into more detail.

Each of the four products suggested is an innovation using the latest technology. They already exist in some form and all, in fact, are likely to be available fairly widely in the near future (the Japanese are close to a workable electric car following a recent breakthrough in battery technology).

Likely customers

Likely customers for (a), (b) and (c) are individual consumers who fall into the innovator or early adopter categories in Rogers' model. Businesses may be interested in (a) (for amusement arcades, pubs, training), (c) (company cars, taxi firms) and (d) (though only large businesses for (d)).

Qualitative research

Qualitative research could be carried out by means of depth interviews or group discussions with demonstrations of the product. This would aim to find out how consumers perceived the new products. Key issues that might need to be addressed in each case could be as follows.

(i)   Do people understand what 'virtual reality' machines are and how they can benefit from them? Are they just toys? Are they in some way immoral or unnatural?

(ii)   Why bother to have a wall mounted LCD TV? Will this mean disrupting the structure of the home with building works? Is the quality of picture better or worse?

(iii)   Isn't the electric car just a joke, like the Sinclair C5?

(iv)   What benefits are there from voice-recognition office dictation systems? Can this system be used in other circumstances, such as for security purposes? Can it be abused?

Quantitative research

Quantitative research would be needed to discover the size of the potential market. Surveys of various types, preferably incorporating a demonstration (a shop survey or hall survey perhaps) could be used. Postal surveys could target purchasers of innovative goods. A test market would eventually need to be set up and evaluated.

Recommendations

Ideally, a combination of qualitative and quantitative techniques, using small-scale and large-scale samples especially targeted towards likely customer, should be used to discover the marketing potential of one of the four products.

47   PRIMARY AND SECONDARY RESEARCH

Research can be classified as either primary or secondary. Secondary research consists of existing research material and is often termed **desk research**. Primary research is new original data collected specifically for a purpose.

Secondary research is often conducted before primary research because of the high cost of primary research and the time it takes to conduct. Secondary sources include the following.

(a)   **Internal data sources,** for example, sales figures, financial data, customer complaints and past research reports. Internal data sources are often a neglected area of marketing research. Sometimes the way the data is collected can make an important difference to their use in marketing research.

(b)   **Government sources.** There are many publications from government departments that are useful secondary research sources. The **guide to official Statistics** (HMSO) and **Regional Statistics** (HMSO) are useful publications that will aid the researcher to discover what statistics are available and where they can be found. Government departments also publish data that may be of use to the market researcher: for example, **Housing and Construction Statistics** and **Family Expenditure Survey Reports.** Government departments in other countries also publish statistical data, as do organisations such as the EU.

(c)   **Other publications.** There is a vast array of additional data sources available to the researcher. Many trade associations publish data for the industry. Yearbooks and directories are published in many industries. Professional institutions also provide members with information. The general and trade press also can be useful sources of information on trends and competitors. There are a number of commercial research companies that can also be used. Well known examples in this area are Mintel, MEAL (Media Expenditure Analysis), Euromonitor and the Economist Intelligence Group. Industry surveys from a financial viewpoint are conducted by some brokerage firms.

Secondary research can be expensive if all these reports are purchased. It may be in the company's best interest to join one of the main commercial libraries for example at London or Manchester Business School. Secondary data has a number of limitations which will be dealt with later; first we will turn our attention to primary research.

To be successful, research should ideally use more than one technique. Secondary data can be used, for example, as an industry overview and to suggest areas where primary research is required. Although comparatively cheap, secondary research does have limitations. It can give an overview of an industry but many of the details that are important to marketing management are missing. There may not be a great deal of secondary information available in certain industry sectors, so primary research becomes more important. If there is data available for the industry as a whole it is not specific to any one company.

In practice some of the secondary data sources can be quite difficult to obtain. The choice of research methods obviously depends on the objectives of the research. If you wish to find out the consumer attitudes to your product, secondary internal sources can be used to a certain degree, but primary research would give a more detailed and useful picture. Primary research is not without problems though, as specialist staff need to be used to administer and analyse primary data. However, the main limitation of secondary research is that it does not specifically relate to the company's consumers.

48 PRIMARY AND SECONDARY DATA

(a) **Primary and secondary data**

Primary data is original data collected using field/primary research techniques by the researcher for the purposes of the project in hand. The data can be collected using questionnaires, observation, experimentation or interviewing respondents qualitatively. In this particular example, questionnaires could be sent to potential purchasers in the European countries in question. Alternatively, agents or experts in the field could be interviewed to find out more about the likely reaction to such a product launch.

Secondary data on the other hand, is data that exists already. It is sourced using desk research techniques. Examples in this case could include the UN Yearbook, Euromonitor (market research) reports, economic digest etc.

Much of the information will be available in this country, either on-line or in libraries (including the Export Marketing Information Centre in London), although it may be necessary to go to the countries in question to obtain more details.

The sort of secondary data required to assess the market for a new product in Europe will relate to the following.

(i)   **Social** factors (demographics, languages spoken and other cultural issues).

(ii) **Legal** factors (import/export restrictions). **Note.** If Europe means EU, there should be no problems; if it includes Central Europe, this may need to be considered in more depth.

(iii) **Economic** factors (economic growth, rates of exchange, inflation, expenditure patterns etc).

(iv) **Political** factors (political stability, attitudes towards foreign companies).

(v)   **Technological** factors (availability of equipment and resources required).

(b) **Uses of secondary data and advantages over primary data**

It is vital that secondary data is considered before launching into field research. There are three key stages where secondary data can be used.

(i)   Initially information will be required to screen each country to assess the opportunities and the risks of launching the new product.

(ii) Having selected the countries which seem the most appropriate, secondary data can be used to analyse the potential for the industry in question in those countries.

(iii) Finally, secondary data can be used to forecast the potential for the company itself.

The advantages that secondary data have over primary data are that it is relatively **cheap, quick** and **easy** to locate.

It is probably easiest to appreciate the advantages of secondary over primary by examining the problems associated with primary research.

(i)   **Expense.** The cost of travel to the country or countries in question and potentially the need to brief several different marketing research agencies.

(ii) **Sampling.** Actually defining a representative sample and locating it may be quite difficult in some countries.

(iii) **Incorrect or non-response.** In some Central and Eastern European countries, there may be suspicion of people asking too many questions (a hangover from the days of the secret police).

(iv) **Language.** Questionnaires need to be translated correctly. It may be necessary to translate them, then have them re-translated back into English to check for errors. Likewise, responses need translating correctly.

(v) **Cultural factors.** Different techniques are better accepted in different countries. In some places it is no longer thought wise or acceptable to interview people in their homes and telephone interviewing may be better; in other places the opposite may be true.

All potential sources of secondary data should therefore be explored before carrying out any primary research as this will certainly help define further research and many even negate the need for it. The only exception to this is if it is deemed necessary to visit the countries in question to collect secondary data, in which case it may be worth interviewing a few 'experts' while there.

49 RESEARCH TECHNIQUES

> **Tutorial note.** It is assumed in the context of this question that shopping mall tests refer to mall intercept surveys and not hall tests.

REPORT

To: Marketing Director, Airdirect
From: R. Unway, Consultant
Date: December 6 2000
Subject: Alternative marketing research techniques

Three alternative marketing research techniques and their appropriateness to achieving the stated objectives will be briefly discussed, but firstly we need to identify respondents.

Respondents will need to be drawn from two segments - business users and holiday travellers. These can be further sub-divided into existing or non-users of the airline. If tour operators need to be canvassed, some form of depth interviews would need to be conducted.

(a) **Shopping mall tests**

Shopping mall tests or intercept surveys are carried out in shopping centres or malls in busy town centre areas. They are a form of face-to-face interview. The interviewer takes up a suitable position and makes approaches to potential respondents. Interviews are normally fairly brief, lasting no more than ten minutes. As soon as one interview is completed, the interviewer will seek a new respondent, thereby maximising the number of interviews achieved within a given time.

There are a number of benefits of this type of face-to-face interviewing.

(i) Response rates are relatively high.

(ii) Initial questions can be asked in order to check the suitability of the respondent.

(iii) Use of a structured questionnaire will ensure that questions are asked in the correct order.

(iv) Targets can be set (percentage split between male and female respondents, for example).

(v) The interviewer can check that questions have been understood.

(vi) Respondents can be prompted to answer question fully.

Clearly shopping mall tests would be inappropriate to target business users. They would also seem not entirely appropriate for holiday makers since most people select a package holiday from a tour operator and book through a travel agent. Few travellers purchase 'flight only' tickets, enabling them to fly with a preferred airline. Also, the short questionnaire format of intercept surveys does not lend itself to obtaining the qualitative data (views and opinions) which are being sought.

(b) **Focus groups**

These are groups of individuals (normally 6-10) who are selected to discuss a particular topic in some depth. The members are chosen using strict criteria so as to be representative of the target market. Focus groups are conducted at a suitable location (often a local hotel). A trained moderator guides the discussion and controls any dominant personalities. Focus groups sessions are often recorded for later analysis.

Focus groups are suitable for obtaining qualitative date, particularly at an early stage of the research. Benefits include the following.

(i)   Group interaction stimulates discussions and views.
(ii)   Differences between consumers and their influences are highlighted.
(iii) A cheaper and fuller analysis is obtained than with depth interviews.

Focus groups would seem to be very appropriate for carrying out the airline research. The key target groups of business users and holiday makers can be selected and group sessions can comprise customers, non-customers or a pre-determined mix. The in-depth discussion generated should provide the necessary qualitative data.

There are a number of disadvantages to focus groups, however.

(i)   The sample size will necessarily be limited, which may lead to managers forming premature conclusions.

(ii)   The quality of discussion will depend on a large extent on the skill of the moderator.

(iii) Recruiting representative samples of people may be problematical; in the case of business users, these need to be the decision makers who book or influence the choice of airline reservation.

(iv)   Analysis and interpretation can be difficult.

(c) **Postal questionnaires**

These are questionnaires which are sent to respondents for self-completion. They are often pre-coded to facilitate subsequent analysis. Postal questionnaires are often of a 'tick-box' format for ease of completion. For this reason they lend themselves to quantitative research (obtaining facts and figures). However, some qualitative information can be sought. Postal questionnaires have a low response rate (10% would be considered a good rate of return) and therefore costs can be high if a large sample is needed. However, response rates can be increased by good, clear questionnaire design, the inclusion of a well-composed covering letter, and, in some cases, by pre-testing. Benefits include speed of response and suitability for computer processing.

This technique is worthy of consideration but may not generate the qualitative data sought. Also, some form of incentive, such as a prize draw for a free flight might be necessary to boost the level of response. Questionnaires sent by fax might generate a higher response amongst business users. Holidaymakers would need to be accessed via a suitable commercial database.

Other questionnaire distribution techniques could be considered (such as asking passengers to complete questionnaires during the flight).

50 MOTIVATION RESEARCH

Motivation research became very popular in the 1950s and was enthusiastically adopted by many researchers at that time. Its background is in clinical psychology.

In marketing research, it is used to understand buyer behaviour and what motivates people to act in a certain way. One could try establishing why people buy a particular product or service by asking them straight out, either in a qualitative type interview or a questionnaire. However, they may not be able to answer such a question, as they may not even be aware of their real motivations. Even if they can answer, they may be too embarrassed to give such information, as they may feel their behaviour is irrational or unusual in some way.

Methods such as psychodrama have been developed to help people express their innermost feelings and motivations in an alternative way. Psychodrama (or role playing) involves people acting out different scenarios, for example pretending to buy a particular product or even assuming the role of sales person. It can also be used in a slightly different way in product development by getting people to pretend to be a particular product and thereby giving that product a personality which they project.

Psychodrama is just one type of projective technique and according to Chisnall (1992) has not been used extensively in marketing research as it is difficult to interpret the results. Other techniques which can also be used are given below.

The third person test. Respondents are asked to put themselves in the position of a typical person who might do a particular thing and to comment on that person. The classic example of this was where housewives were asked to look at one of two shopping lists, identical except that one had instant coffee on it and the other filter coffee, and to say what sort of person would have drawn up such a list.

Sentence or story completion tests. Here the respondent is asked to look at an incomplete sentence or story and asked to say what they think comes next. For example, 'people who shop at Robertson's supermarkets are.'

Thematic apperception test. The respondent is shown a series of pictures and asked to tell the story or say how that situation might have arisen. In some cases just one cartoon is shown and the person asked to fill in the speech bubble.

The above examples of motivation research techniques may be used in individual interviews or group sessions.

51 INTERVIEWING METHODS

> **Tutorial note.** The context of the question made it clear that telephone and face-to-face interviewing were to be evaluated, not every conceivable research technique.

MEMORANDUM

To: Julie Roberts
From: Amanda Green
Date: December 2 2000
Subject: Appropriate research strategies and their respective merits

There are three suitable research strategies available to you. All three can provide qualitative data to a greater or lesser extent.

(a)   Face-to-face interviews (either semi-structured, unstructured or depth).
(b)   Group discussions/focus groups.
(c)   Telephone questionnaires.

(a) **Face-to-face interviews**

   (i) **Semi-structured**

Such interviews consist of both open and closed questions. The former give respondents a free choice of response and hence facilitate the gathering of qualitative data. 'Which factors do you consider to be most important in selecting this product?' is an example of such a question. Closed questions have a choice of a number of pre-determined answers. With open questions, further probing questions can be asked to glean more information relating to attitudes and behaviour. For example you could ask 'Why do you consider cost to be the most important factor in selecting a product?'

Probing techniques can be used to gain very specific information from respondents but they require considerable technical interviewing skills.

   (ii) **Unstructured**

Unstructured interviews are not constrained by a formal questionnaire structure but instead interviewers work from a checklist of areas to be covered. The interviewer controls the interview but uses the checklist to ensure that the areas covered are consistent from interview to interview. The technique is highly qualitative and gives respondents the chance to discuss particular issues in some depth. Unstructured interviews are useful both in helping to formulate semi-structured interview formats and in gaining additional qualitative data in areas in which probing questions from semi-structured interviews yielded promising data.

   (iii) **Depth**

These interviews allow deeper levels of thought to be explored. They can uncover deep-seated motives and explain behaviour patterns which semi-structured and unstructured interview techniques cannot reveal.

Their principal merit is that they allow personal material to be discussed to uncover the true motives and attitudes of individuals. There are, however, a number of disadvantages to such interviews. Depth interviews are time consuming; it is seldom possible to conduct more than three or four per day. They are also more costly than group discussions (which will be covered later in this memo).

Generally, face-to-face interviews benefit from allowing two-way communication. Skilled interviewers can observe and evaluate non-verbal communication as well as verbal responses. Interviewers can probe and explain to varying extents. The interview location can be chosen such that respondents feel relaxed and at ease.

(b) **Group discussions** (including focus groups)

Group discussions generally comprise 8-10 respondents with a skilled interviewer (often a trained psychologist) taking the role of group moderator. The moderator ensures that all key issues are discussed without meandering too far from the point. He or she also encourages respondents and regulates any dominant personalities. The sessions can be videoed or taped for later analysis. Group discussions are not expensive to conduct and a number can be conducted over a short period of time. They provide an excellent source of qualitative data which is particularly useful at an early stage of the research since it can assist the design of the programme. They are useful in identifying important variables which need to be explored in greater detail There are a number of other advantages to group discussion.

(i) They establish a non-intimidating environment conducive to obtaining quality responses.

(ii) Group discussions stimulate ideas on the part of other participants and hence a range of attitudes can be studied.

(iii) Social and cultural influences can be evaluated.

A skilled interviewer is essential to moderate proceedings, however.

(c) **Telephone questionnaires**

Telephone research is a faster and more cost-effective means of gathering data compared to face-to-face interviews or group discussions. It is most suited to the collection of relatively small amounts of information, however. Opportunities for qualitative input are therefore limited. The technique has proved particularly useful in industrial research.

The key advantages of telephone questionnaires are as follows.

(i) High probability of locating respondent
(ii) Reasonable co-operation levels
(iii) A wide spectrum of respondents can be contacted
(iv) Open-ended questions are possible
(v) Respondents can be screened for research suitability
(vi) Relatively fast, allowing a considerable number of interviews to be carried out

In summary, all the techniques considered will produce qualitative data. The final choice will depend on the exact nature of the views being sought and the depth of research required. It could, of course, be beneficial to use a combination of the techniques discussed above.

52 TUTORIAL QUESTION: CUSTOMER SATISFACTION

Introduction

The organisation chosen for this research programme is the 'Everyman Newsagents'. This is a small paper shop in a suburban setting some two miles from the City centre. In addition to newspapers and magazines, it stocks a variety of sweets, chocolates, snacks, soft drinks, greeting cards, stationery and popular paperback books. The clientele is primarily local inhabitants, with some passing trade during the morning and evening 'rush hours'. It has never conducted any research into customer satisfaction and has recently changed hands. The new owner has commissioned the study with a view to establishing ways in which the business might be improved.

The aims of the study

(a) An analysis of **historical sales records** could establish actual past levels of sales (and contribution) of the different lines and act as some sort of base line for decisions.

(b) **Questionnaires** have the advantage of producing standardised data which should allow sensible analysis to be made and conclusions to be drawn but they are probably best for factual-type information on purchasing patterns, frequency of visiting and so on. They can be issued to large numbers of customers and so a wide coverage can be obtained.

(c) **In-depth interviews** are much more useful for establishing attitudes, values, opinions and could be used as a way of asking 'hypothetical' questions of the 'what else would you like to see on offer?' type.

(d) **House-to-house visits with interviews and questionnaires** would have the same advantages and limitations as above but would take place at the respondents' home. An added advantage might be the opportunity to question the whole household as opposed to a single 'user'.

(e) **Telephone surveys** are rather more expensive, and could discriminate by eliminating households without a telephone. They do have the advantage of allowing those people who might otherwise be in too much of a hurry when in the shop (such as when on their way to work) to be questioned.

(f) **Focus groups** could prove a useful source of information on the 'desired' image and product range for the outlet.

The chosen design

The plan would be to use a variety of approaches with a view to collecting different types of information.

For existing customers, questionnaires picked up in the shop or sent out with newspaper deliveries could be used. Questions would determine how often and when customers visited the 'Everyman' and what their particular purchasing patterns were. Tick boxes' would aid analysis. Additionally, the questionnaire could have an open-ended section asking about additional products/services that customers might welcome. (These products might include some named possibilities such as National Lottery, filled rolls and sandwiches and there could also be a blank space where customers could nominate particular products). To help improve the response rate, respondents could be asked to fill in names and addresses for entry into a prize draw as a reward for their time.

These names and addresses would also give a useful source of customers from whom a **focus group** could be chosen. This group would meet perhaps just once or twice to brainstorm reaction to current service and to explore the factors that might make the service even more attractive. Armed with these ideas, an interview schedule/questionnaire could be devised which could be the basis of some **face to face interviews**. This would allow a check to be made on the extent to which the group's ideas were shared by a wider audience.

For non-customers, a parallel service of activities could be considered, but in this case the issue is finding people who do not shop at 'Everyman'. A major problem is likely to be identifying a representative sample of such non-customers. Samples may be random, quasi-random (systematic, stratified or multi-stage samples) or non-random (quota or cluster samples). A full census is not feasible within the budgetary constraints of as small business, so a version of **random sampling** should be used, with the community charge register (convenient for identifying the local market) as the sampling frame. Individuals and households should be randomly selected, and any which turn out to be regular customers should be eliminated. While this may lack the formality of stratified, cluster or quota sampling, within the limits of this relatively small exercise reliable results should be obtained cheaply.

Conclusion

This exercise should allow customer and non-customer views of 'Everyman', its service and its range of goods to be determined. Collected in this way, the analysis should be relatively straightforward and uncomplicated to interpret. Any likely suggestions to emerge can then be costed and evaluated in terms of the new owner's objectives and appropriate decisions can be made. It is presumptuous to guess at what these might be - but they could include widening the product base, extending opening hours, training staff in interpersonal and selling skills, or offering additional services such as photocopying and so on.

53 TUTORIAL QUESTION: DATA COLLECTION USING QUESTIONNAIRES

Once it has been decided that quantitative data will be collected using a structured questionnaire, there are various ways in which the questionnaire can be administered.

(a) Face to face in the person's home or office.

(b) Face to face in the street or shopping mall.

(c) Over the telephone (with the interviews either working from home or from a central location).

(d) By post or fax.

(e) Other self-administered (eg in a restaurant, in a hotel room or in a magazine).

(f) Via the Internet (e-mail).

Each of these methods will be looked at in the table below which shows the relative positive and negative points.

Method	Advantages	Disadvantages
(a)	Respondent at ease; body language visible; home/office can be observed; interviewer can explain/probe; long interview possible (up to 1 hr); visual aids can be used; CAPI* can be used.	Growing resistance to letting strangers into one's home; expensive difficult to monitor interviews; may be many interruptions.
(b)	Interviewer can show, probe and explain.	People often in a hurry; many potential interruptions; can be uncomfortable (weather, nowhere to sit etc); sample=people who shop in that locality at that time of day.
(c)	Sample can be chosen randomly; interviewer can probe and explain; CATI* can be used; supervisors can listen in (central location of interviewers)	Difficult to use visual aids unless sent in advance; long interviews not possible; supervisor cannot listen in (if interview from home); respondent may be distracted.
(d)	Similar to postal. May be treated as more urgent (until junk faxes start to annoy)	Similar to postal. Confidentiality could be a problem; only owners of fax machines would be sampled.
(e)	Similar to (d); specialist magazines and journals are good way or researching certain segments.	Sample self selecting and only users; otherwise similar to (d)
(f)	Fast and easy to use; delivery is certain; reasonable cost; flexibility in response (e-mail mail or fax); less paper wasted.	Only reach e-mail subscribers; size of questionnaire may be limited (form configuration); fear of computers.

*CAPI/CATI = Computer Assisted Personal/Telephone Interviewing

As has been shown above, each method has its own strengths and weaknesses and these should be borne in mind when choosing the most appropriate method to use in a survey.

54   RESEARCH SURVEY METHODS

MEMORANDUM

To: Managing Director, Bestbuys Ltd
From: Bob Greenhorn, Marketing Manager
Subject: Consumer research survey methods
Date: December 6 2000

Consumer research is that part of marketing research which involves the systematic gathering, recording and analysing of data about specific consumer issues. In this instance we need to gather data on the attractiveness of our range in terms of product offerings and prices compared to the competition. Off-the-peg research, such as syndicated research available from a research organisation or omnibus research from regular surveys, will not provide the detailed data required. Primary or field research will therefore be required and so we need to commission or undertake made-to-measure research.

The research will need to gather the following type of data on our products and those of our competitors.

(a) Relationship between quality, price, value and associated image.
(b) Price perceptions.
(c) Presentation issues, such as shape, colour, packaging, service levels.
(d) Positioning of products.
(e) Strength of brand/trade name.
(f) Extent of product range and degree of choice offered to different market segments.
(g) Stages within product life cycle.

Clearly there is a need for both quantitative and qualitative data. Various survey methods are available to collect such data and their relative advantages and disadvantages will now be discussed.

(a) **Interview/mall intercept surveys**

Shopping mall tests or intercept surveys are carried out in shopping centres or malls in busy town centre areas. They are a form of face-to-face interview, where the interviewer takes up a suitable position and makes approaches to potential respondents. Interviews are normally fairly brief, lasting no more than ten minutes. As soon as one interview is completed the interviewer will seek a new respondent, thereby maximising the number of interviews achieved within a given time.

Advantages

(i)   Response rates are relatively high.

(ii)   Initial questions can be asked in order to check suitability of the respondent (such as his/her knowledge of the product group).

(iii) use of a structured questionnaire will ensure that questions are asked in the correct order.

(iv)   Targets can be set (the percentage split between male and female respondents, for example).

(v)   The interviewer can check the questions have been understood.

(vi)   Respondents can be prompted to answer questions fully.

Disadvantages

(i)   Not all respondents will have sufficient knowledge of the product in question.

(ii)   Such techniques are not appropriate for in-depth questioning or probing of the answers given, for example to determine the reason for consumer preference.

(b) **In store surveys**

These are similar to mall intercepts surveys but are conducted within specific shops or just outside them.

Advantages

(i)   They are more targeted than intercept surveys (appropriate retailers can be selected) and hence lead to an increase in quality of responses.

(ii)   Recruitment can be pre- or post-purchase by interviewing people entering or leaving the store.

Disadvantages

The permission of the retailer needs to be gained.

(c) **Hall tests**

An extension of the above two survey methods, respondents who use/have experience of the products in question are asked to participate in a survey conducted in a nearby pre-booked location.

Advantages

(i)   Samples, videos, displays and so on can be used to aid data gathering on the product ranges in question.

(ii)   Interviews can be more in-depth.

(iii)   An appropriate environment can be created to help ensure the right quality of responses.

Disadvantages

They are more costly to administer and conduct.

Other types of surveys include in-house (doorstep) interviews and business interviews. The former would be more appropriate for consumer research - interviewers may be given a list of names and addresses or be limited to certain areas. Interviews can be pre-arranged but can be time-consuming. Longer interviews are possible.

(d) **Questionnaires**

These can be administered (telephone questionnaires) or self-administered (postal questionnaires). They can also be sent by fax or e-mail. Questionnaires are often of a tick list format for ease of completion and they allow both quantitative and qualitative data to be sought.

Advantages

(i)   The results are easy to analyse (especially using computer techniques).
(ii)   They can be pre-tested to increase response rates.

Disadvantages

(i)   Postal questionnaires have a low response rate.
(ii)   They may not generate the degree of qualitative data required.

Summary

All the survey techniques listed have particular strengths and weaknesses and it may be that a combination of methods will need to be considered. Focus groups could have a role to play, where issues such as brand identity, perception of quality and so on could be considered in more depth.

55 TUTORIAL QUESTION: VALUE OF CUSTOMER SURVEYS

MEMORANDUM

To: Marketing Director
From: Marketing Assistant
Date: December 8 2000

Customer surveys - how to make them a more reliable method of measuring customer attitudes, motivations and decisions

Following on from our earlier discussion about whether respondents tell the truth when taking part in customer surveys the following is a reflection of some of the issues relevant to any future decisions.

1 Respondent truthfulness

Your assertion that respondents seldom tell the truth is undoubtedly correct in some instances. The reasons for such behaviour are many and varied.

- Respondents may give the quickest answer wanting to get away.

- They are not comfortable with their own behaviour so they don't tell the truth in order to avoid embarrassment (especially if the truth is not politically correct).

- Unconsciously they change their attitude because of being asked officially - ie an example of the Hawthorne effect.

- They may not know the answer to a question, but are unwilling to admit ignorance and so they make up an answer.

- They are under the influence of interviewer and wish to please.

- They may give the 'expected' or 'socially acceptable' answer.

- They may not care.

- They may be subject to peer pressure.

- They may lack self awareness about their own motivations and so be unable to answer truthfully.

2 Overcoming the problems

It is very difficult to create customer surveys which would be able to eliminate all those factors and provide us with objective, truthful answers in every case. However there are methods which can decrease the possibility of truth distortion in customer surveys.

Firstly there are issues concerning those who are asked to respond and this is a question of the **sampling** approach to be adopted. It is an issue that impacts on the likely truthfulness of some, but, more importantly, the validity of any conclusions reached.

Secondly there are issues concerning **survey design** which can help the problem and assist in eliminating untruthfulness.

- Commencing with suitable factual, classification questions that may allow certain classifications to be treated as being less reliable at the analysis stage (eg eliminating bachelors from babycare questionnaires unless they can 'prove' experience).

- Approaching the question via a variety of techniques - eg closed questions with a yes/no response; open ended questions allowing narrative response; Likert scales allowing graded response.

- Asking basically the same question more than once to test the robustness of responses.

- Utilising techniques where the 'right' answer is not obvious (forced choice of adjectives, repertory grid etc).

- Using methods like work associations, ending sentences which can show consumer preference.

- Use of semi-permanent panels where extended contact could breed trust, confidence and honesty.

- The elimination of interviewer bias (by choosing the non-personal methods such as the mail).

- If we do use interviewers, using well trained interviewers.

- The careful interpretation of the data can also eliminate the less reliable results.

If you would wish to discuss this in more detail in order to establish how we might improve our present practice I would be happy to expand these ideas.

56   SECONDARY SOURCES OF DATA

> **Tutorial note.** Obviously it is best to choose a business sector that you know something about yourself; then you are likely to be familiar with the data that is available, since you will be using it yourself in your job.

Introduction

This answer will focus on a Japanese financial services organisation looking to retail investment products to the UK market.

Marketing research

This is the systematic and objective collection of information to be used in the decision making process. It does not exist on its own, but will be used in conjunction with other management information (financial, operations etc) to develop the organisation's strategic plans.

There are different types of research - primary and secondary, field and desk, qualitative and quantitative. In this scenario we are focused on secondary research which consists of analysing existing data, reports and research. (Primary research, in contrast, is concerned with first-hand commissioned surveys, questionnaires and interviews and is much more time consuming and expensive.)

Sources of secondary data

The prime source of secondary data for the financial services sector is that produced by the government.

Government statistics

Relevant information would include the following.

(a)   Trade cycle statistics. Is the economy in recession or boom? Where are we in the trade cycle? Which phase are we likely to be moving into? Ideally it could be most advantageous to time the entry into the market to coincide with the recovery phase.

BPP PUBLISHING

(b)   Interest rate levels (historical and current so that predictions may be made).

(c)   Inflation rates.

(d)   Employment levels (significant for predicting disposable income).

(e)   Population data via census statistics.

Other sources

Numerous other sources exist, including the following.

(a)   The Personal Investment Authority, which regulates companies offering investment products.

(b)   The Association of British Insurers, who can provide information on the numbers of different investment products available, market share, sales figures, and other significant and relevant information concerning this specific market.

(c)   Reuters, the international information service.

(d)   Extel, which provides information on specific companies (ie the potential competition).

(e)   The Stock Exchange TOPIC facility can provide information on stock markets, exchange rates, levels of investment activity etc.

(f)   Trade and specialist journals such as:

- Financial Adviser
- Money Marketing
- Money Management
- What Investment?
- Investors Chronicle
- Economist

(g)   Quality newspapers, particularly the Financial Times will also give economic and business commentaries as well as current unit prices of investment products. They may also be a potent source of information on significant political trends (the stability of the government, dates of general elections, reports on political opinion polls, possible policy shifts and so on).

Conclusion

The sources of secondary data listed will need to be considered in the light of the relevance and reliability of the information.

Such material may be very volatile and so particular attention will have to be paid to **when** the data was collected - adjustments may then need to be made in the light of subsequent occurrences. The basis of calculations may have to be examined - for instance there has been some criticism of the way in which government employment figures have been calculated (and also the numerous changes in the methods of calculation) which could be misleading and disguise the true levels of unemployment.

The different sources will provide different qualities of data which will be of significance at different stages of the decision making process.

Thus the Japanese company might be well advised to start with a basic appraisal of the UK economy and the trade cycle before moving on to consider the political framework. Next an analysis of the financial and investment services market would be appropriate, before leading on to an examination of the competition and the market opportunities and specific competitive advantages which might exist.

One other option which might be considered is to commission a reputable business school or market analyst to gather the specialised secondary data on behalf of the company.

57   MARKET INTELLIGENCE

Market Intelligence

Given the situation described in the question (an established company contemplating entry into the UK market), I would consider a number of sources for information on possible competitors. The majority of the information would come from secondary (already existing) sources and research.

(a) **In-house desk research**. If we are already an established figure in other markets we will have considerable information regarding competitors in other markets. Given this knowledge we can establish whether the same competition is operating in the UK.

(b) **Relevant electronic databases** could be purchased, or on-line facilities subscribed to.

(c) **Government statistics** from Department of Trade and Industry, Department for Education and Employment and so on, will give data on market activities and employment patterns in specific and relevant industries.

(d) **Market research publications** such as Mintel, Keynote, Euromonitor, Datamonitor, from these I would hope to gain information on the market profile, the market players, product positioning and market shares.

(e) **Trade journals** of the particular market would be scanned to identify the marketing activity of competitors, hints as to future plans, new product offerings and so on. Some of this information would come from articles and editorials, other from analysis of advertisements.

(f) Having identified the key players it is possible to gain access to the **company accounts** of those public companies via Companies House. This should yield data on sales turnover, staffing levels, locations, capital expenditure and so on.

(g) **Patent and Trade Mark applications** could be a useful source of information on developments and innovations.

(h) **Competitive benchmarking** against what is on the market. Information to be gathered from customer surveys, supplier surveys and promotional material.

(i) Considerable information could be gleaned by visiting **Trade Exhibitions** and seeking data on sponsorship involvement. Similarly, informal contacts as relevant conferences may yield valuable information.

(j) **Job advertisement pages** could give an insight into skills being recruited in competitors' companies. This could give indications of possible development projects.

(k) Trawling the **Internet** could give a great deal of data and summaries of similar research exercises.

Observations

As mentioned in the introduction, the secondary research approaches outlined above fall into two broad categories - those which are internal desk research and those which are external to your organisation. Internally we may have more influence to seek clarification and interpretation of data. It may also be possible to check the reasons for the original collection of the information which will allow some evaluation of reliability, age-decay and possible 'political' slants. This last may sometimes be deduced by establishing who conducted the research and for whom it was undertaken. All of these factors are significant limitations when interpreting secondary data.

The information gathered externally is less able to be interrogated in the same way and so care must be taken to get more than a single source to confirm any conclusions that may be drawn. In the UK Government statistics are considered relatively reliable and are usually clearly dated. It is not always clear, however, how long before publication the data was collected so due care must be taken.

Having established the basic information the organisation would be in a much stronger position to commission relevant and pertinent primary research.

58 DATA COLLECTION

> **Tutorial note.** This was a very straightforward question. Do not forget the context of the lecture; indicate timings, variety, exercises, overheads and so on.

If I am preparing a lecture for marketing students I shall assume that they have a basic knowledge of the subject and its terminology. I shall prepare overheads and handouts to avoid tedious note taking and shall attempt to lighten the lecture with anecdotes, an occasional joke and a brief exercise.

The overall plan of the session would be as follows.

(a) Introduction.
(b) Secondary methods of data collection: definitions and sources.
(c) Primary methods of data collection: definitions and sources.
(d) Examples of secondary methods: group to identify advantages and disadvantages.
(e) Examples of primary methods: group to identify advantages and disadvantages.
(f) Exercise.
(g) Review and conclusions.

In more detail, key points would include the following.

Introduction

Marketing intelligence is the cornerstone of successful marketing activities. It involves the collection of relevant data to allow sound decision making by marketing managers, and is the basis for well-informed and sensible managerial decisions. Commonly a distinction is drawn between primary and secondary research (data collection methods), although both have sub-sets and both contribute to the necessary database for sound decision making. This could be illustrated diagrammatically as follows.

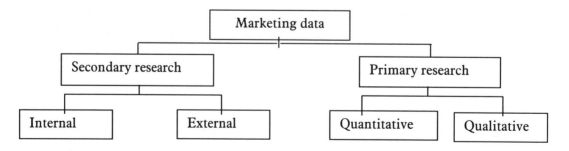

Secondary research

(a) Often known as 'desk research' and involves the collection and analysis of already existing data.

(b) Usually (always?) done **before** primary research is undertaken.

(c) Internal sources

    (i)   Sales reports
    (ii)   Production reports
    (iii) Past company accounts
    (iv) Previous market research reports
    (v)   Research & development reports
    (vi) Sales force reports

(d) External sources

    (i)   Census
    (i)   DTI
    (ii)   Libraries
    (iv) Professional journals
    (v)   Trade reports
    (vi) Embassies
    (vii) Credit agencies
    (viii) Commercial databases
    (ix) The Internet

(e) **Advantages**

    (i)   Can help identify useful areas for primary research

    (ii)   May help develop ideas for product/service innovation

    (iii) Gives essential background information on the area and a knowledge of previously-conducted research

    (iv) Relatively cheap

(f) **Disadvantages**

    (i)   Could be biased

    (ii)   May have been conducted/commissioned for a particular purpose which is not obvious and which could lead to manipulation

    (iii) May be out of date

Primary research

(a) Is tailor-made/designed to meet a specific marketing need.

(b) Observational methods

    (i)   Personal
    (ii)   Mechanical
    (iii) Electronic (eg EPOS)

(c) Survey methods

    (i)   Questionnaires (often interviewed)
    (ii)   Structured interviews
    (iii) Telephone surveys (now commonly computer aided)
    (iv) Postal Surveys

(d) Distinction between quantitative (numerical, factual, 'hard' data) and qualitative (attitudinal, values, emotional data) research.

(e) Focus groups are a specific and growing source of qualitative data which operate on a small sample, but which offer much greater 'depth' of information.

Answer bank

(f) **Advantages**

    (i)   Specifically designed to generate the required data

    (ii)   Can reach a large audience and hence produce a more representative sample

    (iii)   Up-to-date

(g) **Disadvantages**

    (i)   Needs specialist expertise to design and interpret

    (ii)   Can be time consuming to design, conduct and analyse

    (iii)   Expensive

Exercises

This will be a simple group discussion along the following lines.

'You are thinking of opening a restaurant in your locality. Identify the secondary and primary research which you might conduct to help your key decision making.'

I would allow only ten minutes for the discussion, with ten minutes for playback using a flipchart to summarise the key suggestions.

Conclusion

Revisit summary overhead, emphasising key points.

Any questions.

Thanks.

59   DATA FOR OVERSEAS EXPANSION

MEMO

To: Marketing Director
From: Marketing Assistant
Date: December 8 2000
Subject: K data sources

Further to our recent meeting I present below the information you requested.

As we are seeking to expand and develop our UK activities, we need to establish the state of the UK economy, society and market. We will seek to conduct a PEST analysis via an external assessment of the following aspects.

(a) **Political**   - stability
                   - constraints on investment

(b) **Economic**   - state of the national economy
                   - GDP/GNP gross and per head
                   - infrastructure costs, taxation, grants

(c) **Social**   - lifestyles
                   - religion/ethics
                   - demographics
                   - pressure groups

(d) **Technology** - research and development
                   - energy resources
                   - labour force skills
                   - environmental impact

We therefore need **economic research**, which is the broad study of the economy of the country, region, industry and market to establish the key economic aspects. The data obtained may be quite detailed since such research is intended to give insight into the current and future state of the economy under consideration. We will require **secondary research** which, although being somewhat less exciting and 'sexy' than field research, is a very important part of marketing research and is concerned with collecting, analysing and interpreting data which already exists and which is relevant to the organisation and its environment.

Sources of secondary data

It will be simplest to use **published statistics,** which are usually divided into governmental and non-governmental.

Examples of **government statistics** include publications such as the following.

(a) **Census** - numbers and location of the population

(b) **Household Survey** and **Family Expenditure Survey** - giving valuable data on spending patterns

(c) **Annual Abstract of Statistics** - data on housing, population, manufacturing output and so on

(d) **Economic Trends** - gives economic analysis and indicators

(e) **Department of Employment Gazette** - is concerned mainly with employment patterns but contains useful data on, for example, earnings levels for areas and industries

(f) **Business Monitor** - gives information on specific industries

Examples of non-governmental sources include the following.

- Chambers of commerce
- Trade Associations
- Banks
- Kelly's
- CIM
- Financial Times Business Information Service
- Kompass
- News Agencies
- Mintel
- Various websites

Each provides reviews and data on various industries, sectors and localities.

Our project would initially be concerned with **environmental scanning** ('keeping one's ears to the ground'). We therefore need to be aware of what is going on in the marketplace and we may have to keep an eye on competitors as well as maintain a more wide-ranging sensitivity to what is going on in political, social, economic, technological and legal circles. Thus we would be concerned with the following.

(a) **Market research.** A more detailed study of a market to identify total demand (usually for all products or services under consideration). It aims to establish how the market is changing, growing and contracting, the competitors in the market, market shares, prices, and factors which may influence the market and its development.

(b) **Demand studies.** Detailed in-depth study of the demand for specific products and services in order to obtain an up-to-date picture of what is happening to demand for the products/services in question.

(c) **Competitor research.** Detailed study of the competition - what they are doing, what products/services they are offering, how and why they are succeeding (or not). This can lead to a 'competitor profile' which may be used to predict likely competitor reaction to action, changes or innovations.

The following are therefore the required secondary data sources for this stage of the process.

(a) Trade journals eg Campaign, Marketing.
(b) Specialist magazines such as the Economist.
(c) Specialist press such as the Financial Times.
(d) Academic journals such as the Harvard Business Review.

Additional sources of data could include the following.

(a) Conferences and exhibitions.

(b) Networking (including contacts with competitors, examining their products, financial statements, press releases, job advertisements and so on).

In terms of structuring a report on the specific market we are seeking to enter, I would suggest using the Porter model, which focuses on five key forces acting on an organisation.

(a) The power of competitors.
(b) The power of buyers.
(c) The power of suppliers.
(d) The threat of potential entrants to the market.
(e) The threat posed by substitute products.

Once we have established the broad viability of the market we could look at more specific information via use of secondary data which could include bought-in information from **consumer panels** and **retail panels.** This would allow us to expand into more specific customer, product, sales, distribution and promotional research before committing ourselves to expensive and highly-specialised primary research.

60 NEW PRODUCT RESEARCH

To: T. Ipsy, Sales and Marketing Director
From: T. Iddly, Marketing Manager
Date: December 8 2000

New product launch

The **steps** that would need to be undertaken are as follows.

(a) **Definition of the objectives of the research**

These would relate to the three areas detailed:

(i)   Acceptability.
(ii)   Forecasts.
(iii) Pricing strategy.

(b) Identification of suitable sources of data and collection techniques relating to the three areas mentioned in (a) above.

(i)   In assessing the **acceptability** of the new product, primary research will be required and it is likely that qualitative techniques will be more helpful than quantitative, as feelings and opinions need to be gauged.

(ii)   There are three different types of primary research techniques that could be used to assess what the market thinks.

(1) **Depth interviews.** These consist of one-to-one interviews with members of the target group lasting between 1 and 2 hours. They are useful to find out more about what motivates people and what they feel about different things. As no-one else is present, weaker people are not swayed by others as they might be in group discussions. As a general opinion on the drink's acceptability or otherwise is required, this is less likely to be used here.

(2) **Focus groups.** Groups of 6-10 individuals from the target age range (18-30 year olds) would need to be recruited. They would then be invited to a suitable venue (ideally with one-way mirrors and recording equipment) so that proceedings could be observed. Discussions would be led by a trained moderator who would be briefed to ascertain what the participants look for in a drink and what they think of the new product (samples would be provided). Alternatively, samples might be provided before hand and then participants asked at a later date to discuss the drink.

(3) **Test marketing.** Either the product could be launched on a trial basis in a particular area or a promotional evening could be arranged at a typical drinking venue frequented by target consumers. People could be offered a free/cheap drink on condition that they answer a few brief questions about it afterwards. They could also be asked how likely they would be to buy the product. This information could help in formulating the forecasts. People may say they like a new product but not necessarily want to buy it.

(iii) To **forecast** future sales, a certain amount of secondary research will be required in order to ascertain the total market for alcoholic drinks, the percentage consumed by 18-30 year olds and the market shares of the competition. Asking participants in the qualitative research about their intention to buy is another method of gaining information on which to base forecasts.

(iv) The **pricing strategies** of the competition will also need to be looked at. There are different ways of setting prices, and although production and development costs much be recouped, it is not sufficient to know ones own costing structure. The price that the market will stand is probably the best guide in this sort of fashion market.

(c) **Data collection.** To be able to complete this stage, suitable samples representative of the target audience will need to be located.

(d) **Data analysis.** Interpretation of qualitative research takes training and experience. Analysis of market shares and competitive pricing ideally requires a spreadsheet package.

(e) **Presentation of results.** Key findings, including opinions of the target consumers, forecasts of what they are likely to buy and at what price, will all need to be presented to the Marketing Director and possibly other members of the Board.

Assuming the product is launched, further research will be needed to check that the product is still popular, that the forecasts are on target and that the pricing strategy is correct.

61 NEW PRODUCT MARKET RESEARCH

The following report outlines the market research plan to be conducted prior to the launch of our new magazine aimed at teenage females.

Research conducted last year revealed the UK female teenage market as a viable new market for our magazine publications. The secondary research carried out at this time has defined a demographic and psychographic profile of our target market.

The following plan has been developed for **pre-launch research** into the market to define the most successful product characteristics, pricing and advertising support. As a wealth of secondary research has already been gathered, this plan will focus entirely on primary sources of information.

The plan is structured to cover each stage in the standard research process. Sections therefore cover the following areas:

- Define the research objectives
- Ascertain the best methods for obtaining the information
- Collect the data
- Process the data
- Make recommendations
- Implement the recommendations

Research Objectives

Research objectives must be devised to be specific, measurable, actionable, reasonable and timescaled (ie SMART). Suggested objectives for the research are as follows.

- To investigate attitudes to magazine content and layout styles amongst the target group, to discover the most appropriate product mix

- To investigate attitudes to advertising message and content amongst the target group to discover the most appropriate advertising mix

- To quantify media consumption of the target group

- To investigate attitudes to magazine pricing amongst the target group

Methods for obtaining information

There are two appropriate primary research methods which could be used to obtain qualitative data of this type. These methods are discussed in the sections below.

Focus Groups

This is a research method which should be given consideration. In this method, a group of six to ten respondents from the target group is engaged in a group discussion with a moderator. Typically, the sessions are recorded or videoed through a two way mirror for later analysis. This format of research allows elements to be evaluated, such as advertising visuals, magazine layouts etc.

Hall tests

The usual format of this method is to recruit respondents from the target group on the street and to invite them to a nearby research room to view material and test their reactions. This could also be combined with a short interview. This method would allow props to be used and appropriate qualitative data could be developed.

The recommendation is to use focus groups for this research for the following reasons:

- It is a more cost effective way of gathering respondent data, leading to larger number of respondents being involved within the budget

- The recording of focus groups allows more in depth analysis of the discussion

- The target group is more likely to 'open up' in a group

- There are potential legal and/or moral implications surrounding street recruitment of this target group

Collect the data

The first issue to consider is that of sampling. Although we have defined demographic and psychographic profiles of the target group, it is recommended that we address geographic considerations for the sample. Previous research projects have used specific city locations in the North, Midlands and South East of the UK to mirror the UK population. It is suggested that this research uses the same locations.

Respondents will be recruited through snowballing techniques which could be achieved through schools and colleges within the target areas. We must also consider the legal and moral implications of respondent recruitment. We will need to gain parental permission and possibly parental accompaniment for the respondents.

Process the data

Discussions will be captured on video. Transcripts of discussions will be produced and qualitative analysis techniques applied to the results.

Recommendations

The results will be written into a report format and a presentation given to company directors and marketing management.

Resources/Costs/Timing issues

We do not have the in-house expertise to conduct a research project of this type. A research brief will be written and submitted to two external marketing research companies. Previous experience would suggest that the budget of £30,000 will finance recruitment, data collection, analysis and reporting of 15 focus groups. The likely timescale for this project is 2 months from the awarding of the contract.

62 PROJECTIVE TECHNIQUES

Along with depth interviews, projective techniques are a set of methods derived from psychoanalytic theory and applied to marketing. Like depth interviews, these techniques are designed to determine motives that are difficult to express or identify. Researchers cannot always ask direct questions, as consumers may not be able to answer, as they are unaware of their motives. Instead, consumers are given a situation, a cartoon, or a set of words and asked to respond. They project their feelings and concerns about product to this less threatening or involving situation.

In one famous experiment in the late 1940s, Haire used a projective technique to discover why women were reluctant to purchase instant coffee, when it was first introduced. He constructed two shopping lists that were identical, except that one included regular coffee and the other instant coffee. Housewives then were asked to project the type of woman most likely to have developed each shopping list. The housewife who included instant coffee in the list was characterised ads lazy and a poor planner. These findings, demonstrated that many women had a deep seated fear of buying products like instant coffee or instant cake mixes because of a concern that their husbands would feel they were avoiding their traditional role as homemakers. As a result of the study, instant coffee was advertised in a family setting portraying the husband's approval. The study, while old, is a classic example of a psychoanalytically oriented approach to the determination of consumer motives.

Motivational research was subject to much criticism when it was first introduced because of its use of indirect methods to determine consumer motives. In fact, there was some question as to whether deep-seated motives could or indeed should be used in marketing and advertising. Nonetheless, motivational research did provide methodological contributions by introducing depth interviews and projective techniques to the study of consumer behaviour.

63   MASS CUSTOMISATION

INTERNAL REPORT – MASS CUSTOMISATION

To: C. Arking, Managing Director
From: B. Eginner, Marketing Assistant
Date: September 6 2000

Introduction

Mass customisation is the creation of individually-designed products and services, tailored to the precise requirements of the individual customer, whilst minimising the cost implications, so that the economies of mass production scale can be sustained. For example, we offer 7 variants of our most popular model, but may still not supply the mixture of features, which entirely meets the expectations of some customers. They may want, for example, a two-door car with automatic transmission, but are faced with a choice between a two-door version with automatic transmission and a four-door with automatic transmission. Listed below are interpretations of several comments that have been made in response to the development of mass customisation:

Marketing opportunity

Here are two examples of organisations which have successfully implemented mass customisation. Black & Decker completely redesigned its power tool product lines, twice, to take advantage of component-sharing modularity to greatly reduce costs whilst providing more variety and speedier product development.

The Levi Personal Pair service enables customers to pay a surcharge and have jeans made to order from over 4 000 permutations of different measurements. In the manufacturing plant, the denim is cut by computer controlled machines and then shipped direct to the retailer or direct to the customer.

Threat

The success of this concept in the car industry depends on cultivating the car prosumer. The prosumer participates in the design of their vehicle at a workstation in the dealership. Using the car manufacturer's CAD/CAM software, the prosumer can first select a combination of body structures and various components that have been tested for safety and performance. Many features of the car can be custom-designed, depending on how much the customer wants to pay.

The above may sound like science fiction but it is in fact taken from plans published by Nissan at the beginning of this decade. If Nissan were considering this concept almost ten years ago then perhaps we are rather late in entering this discussion. As such the threat may come from ignoring the potential of mass customisation.

Passing fad

In some respects, mass customisation is merely the next stage in the development of new manufacturing technologies. In other ways, however, mass customisation is revolutionary rather than incremental: it requires change throughout a company, much more rigorous and focused marketing strategies, a close identification with current (and predicted) customer tastes, highly developed distribution systems and a fresh appraisal of key components within the new value chain. As such it seems unlikely that this is a passing fad.

Illusion

There are many areas where mass customisation is already well-developed: PCs, insurance policies, shampoos, vitamins, clothing, bicycles etc. Equally there are others where acceptance of the need for mass customisation has still some way to go. Furniture is a classic instance where customers are frequently told that their preferred choices are unavailable or incapable of being supplied because they are not in the catalogue. Mass customisation is not an illusion in many areas, however, in all but the premium end of the car market, it has yet to be implemented.

Conclusion

The argument continues to rage about whether it is still legitimate to segment customers into large groups unified against only one dimension or whether segmentation is now dead and has been superseded by the ultimate segment of one; the individual customer.

On the negative side, one-to-one marketing is very difficult to initiate and achieve. The examples that have been discussed above have generally built themselves around the concept from scratch. For mass customisation to work, organisations have to go through four key processes.

- Identify individual customers
- Differentiate those customers
- Interact with the customers
- Redesign the product or service to reflect each customer's specific needs and wants

The benefits of mass customisation could include competitive advantage leading to higher profits, increased market share and delighted customers. The risks could include high development costs that result in expensive, tailor made cars that are not wanted or required by the market.

I hope that this report has provided you with an outline of the information that you require and I look forward to discussing its contents with you at our next meeting.

64 ATTITUDE FORMATION AND CHANGE

1 Definitions

An attitude can be defined as a relatively consistent, learned predisposition to behave in a certain way in response to a given object. Allport offers a more technical definition of an attitude as "a mental and neural state of readiness, organised through experience, exerting a directive or dynamic influence upon the individuals' response to all objects and situation with which it is related".

2 Principal theories

There are a variety of theories surrounding the ways in which attitudes are formed and changed. The following represents a selection:

2.1 Formation

As attitudes are learned pre-dispositions, individuals are motivated to form attitudes in four key ways: by seeking rewarding objects and avoiding negative ones; by protecting self-concept; by expressing core values and making sense of the environment.

Attribution theory describes attitude formation as a product of individuals' interpretations of their own experiences. They make inferences about the causes of their own behaviour and that of others and hence an attitude is formed.

Three major attitude theories emerged in the 1940s and 50s that highlighted the concept of cognitive consistency. They suggested that individuals seek consistency on three levels. Firstly consistency between held attitudes, secondly consistency between attitudes and perceptions of reality and finally consistency between behaviour and self-image.

The difficulty arises when inconsistencies occur and the individual experiences conflict. The means to address this conflict is to change one attitude so that it is compatible with another attitude or behaviour. The next section will consider three consistency theories.

2.2 Change

The balance theory is concerned with what happens when one individual receives information from another. The conflict arises when the individual's attitude to another is negative or their attitude to the object is negative. A positive individual and a positive object result in congruity, any other combination will lack this balance. This theory has been criticised as being too simplistic as the terms negative and positive fail to address the depth of feeling.

Osgood and Tannenbaum's congruity theory addresses this issue of depth by measuring the intensity of positive or negative attitudes on a scale of −3 to +3. Congruity theory states that for consistency to be achieved there has to be an adjustment of both evaluations towards each other until their ratings are the same.

Feistinger's cognitive dissonance theory deals with the discomfort feeling experienced when an individual receives new information that appears to contradict an already held attitude. As a result of this process the individual will seek to address this feeling in a number of ways:

- Making the decision more attractive, perhaps by seeking supportive information
- Devaluing the credibility of the information source
- Devaluing the held attitude
- Changing the attitude to fit with the new information
- Revoking the decision, perhaps by returning a product

3   Application

The chosen scenario is persuading smokers to abandon smoking altogether or to transfer to some form of nicotine substitute. Positive attitudes regarding smoking may have been formed in a variety of ways. The smoker may feel no adverse physical symptoms or may know of individuals who are elderly and have smoked for a considerable period of time with no apparent effects. They may find the chemical composition of cigarettes provides them with a rewarding experience. Many individuals claim that smoking can have a calming influence and may act as an appetite suppressant. In combination, these types of factors may help to form positive attitudes. These can be reinforced in the media with well-known individuals who are successful, slim and attractive being seen smoking. This may reinforce the perception that smoking is glamorous and hence this may reinforce a self-image of sophistication.

A plethora of medical reports and government led initiatives have positively indicated that smoking is harmful to the smoker and those around them. This information will clearly conflict with the type of beliefs discussed above and so result in cognitive dissonance. This may result in actions such as:

- Trying to give up or seek an alternative and so accepting the information and discarding previously held beliefs

- Disbelieving the information source – an organisation would say that, they have a substitute product on the market

- Indicating that the habit can be stopped at any time and that control lies with the individual

Established attitudes are extremely difficult to change for the reasons outlined above. In the case of smoking, behavioural changes are resulting in reduced numbers of smokers. Thus enhancing the peer group pressure effect. However, in this scenario the key is the credibility of the source and the extent to which there is unequivocal evidence that is repeated in a variety of media. This is likely to encourage a change in long held beliefs so that when further information becomes available there is less opportunity for cognitive dissonance.

65 TUTORIAL QUESTION: DELIGHTING CUSTOMERS

(a) In the historical context, marketing as we now know it has gone through a number of phases. Initially, with an excess of demand, the markets tended to be product led. Later, with the growth of communication channels a selling pattern emerged. Later still, our current notion of marketing - concerning satisfaction of customer needs - developed.

The question implies a further development beyond satisfaction into the notion of 'delight'.

To explore this idea we may observe that the key concepts defining such changes are:

- Supply and demand
- Competition
- Customer expectation

The logic supports the implication highlighted as customers, faced with organisations competing for their business in a world characterised by over-supply, become ever more choosy and 'picky'. As competitors attempt to outdo each other to gain the sale, so the customers' expectations rise beyond pure satisfaction. We go beyond the 'must haves', into the 'more ofs', and, ultimately into the area of 'delight'.

However, this movement may not be universal as in some cases customers want to be delighted but in other cases it is less evident. One example recently was carried out by First Direct (a subsidiary of Midland Bank), where a survey showed that over 80% of customers were extremely satisfied with the service they received from First Direct. Whereas only 60% were satisfied with the service from Midland Bank. Bearing in mind that they are essentially one and the same we might wonder how such differences emerge.

The answer may lie in whether we are speaking of a:

- High involvement purchase; or a
- Low involvement purchase.

High involvement purchases will involve considerable research and comparisons while low involvement tends to be the routine re-buy (this could account for the First Direct/Midland results).

The trend seems to be supported in the high involvement field with the advent of 'mass customisation' - eg. Dell Computers, Raleigh Cycles, Levi Jeans producing individually tailored computers, mountain bikes and jeans respectively. Similarly, high involvement decisions such as holidays lend themselves much more easily to the concept of 'delight' than do more mundane purchases such as toilet tissue.

However, the trend is less well marked in low involvement decisions although the offer of supermarkets to do your shopping for you via the Internet could be the sign of things to come. Some sectors are relatively untouched by such ideas of personalisation of service - dustbin collection, distress purchases (petrol on the motorway etc.) but the advent of more competition could change expectations dramatically.

Ultimately, I suspect that competition will lead more and more sectors down this particular road.

(b) If people increasingly move toward the need to be delighted rather than merely satisfied and want products and services tailored to their specific needs, then more and more organisations will move towards mass customisation and it would have far reaching implications for customer segmentation.

Traditionally segmentation is carried out on such aspects as **age**, sex, geographical location, social class etc. In the scenario proposed, this approach seems less and less appropriate - as, if consumers want goods and services to be more specific, then customer segmentation will have to be more specific.

For instance if your company deals in hair colorants and a consumer wants a specific colour that is very rare then you will need to satisfy this consumer or she will change manufacturers and buy the hair colorant off someone who **can** provide the specific colour. This woman/women may be amongst a minority but this minority will account for a certain section of the population, could be the innovator/opinion leader and would have to be segmented accordingly.

There is an inevitable clash between segmentation and individuality. Although Tesco have announced a long term aim (backed by detailed records of purchasing patterns via loyalty card records) of developing the 'segment of one'.

So long as we have competition and an excess of product/service such trends and tensions will continue.

66 CHANGES IN CUSTOMER BEHAVIOUR AND EXPECTATIONS

> **Tutorial note.** You are asked to produce outline notes for the presentation - so there is no need to go for essay format.

NOTES FOR PRESENTATION - 'MARKETING IN 2005'

Hardware required: OHP; slide projector; slides showing examples of products and advertisements; flip chart/pens; handout notes.

Presentation notes	Aids
Introduction Define marketing, product/service Emphasise problems of looking into the future and the lack of reliability and accuracy of predictions Accuracy of predictions Specific problems of 'futurology'	OHPs
Brainstorming session on their perceptions of likely changes	Flip chart

Presentation notes
General issues
Increasing rates of technological change
Changing markets - local/global
Rising consumer expectations - eg health care
New communication channels - internet etc
Speed of communication
Ecological concerns especially pollution
Ethical issues
Demographic changes - older population
Increasing life expectancy
High levels of unemployment
'Haves' and 'have nots' - the 30/30/40 society
Lack of secure long term jobs
'Decline of 'the career'
Decline of socialist/centralist policies especially Welfare State provisions
Growth of competition

Brainstorming session on their perceptions of additional changes

Flip chart

Changes in marketing of existing product/services

OHPs

Economies of scale
Economic power of the large enterprise
Growth of multi-nationals
Growth of 'global products' eg Macdonald's, Toyota
Need to tailor the global to the local market eg Nescafe
Improved and more sophisticated segmentation
Use of EPOS systems to identify individual consuming patterns
Customer care extending into new areas such as education, utilities, etc
Virtual reality technology for advertising and shopping
Internet advertising and shopping

Brainstorming session on their perceptions and ideas

Flip chart

New products and services
Possible growth of the 'black economy' for the 'have nots'
Return to personal services (housekeepers/cleansers/cooks/childminders/
nannies) especially by the 'have nots' for the 'haves'
Internet/TV medical diagnosis
More financial services providing for pensions/care of the elderly/sickness
Insurance as the Welfare State is eroded
Demand for medical services will expand and enlarge
Virtual reality leisure pursuits
Growth of exotic leisure for the 'haves' and wealthy retired
Growth of 'mass customisation' at top end of the market in specialist
Technological areas such as computers, off-road cycles etc

Brainstorming session on their perceptions of likely changes

Flip chart

Disappearance of current products and services
Continuing pressure on sole traders in competition with supermarkets,
greengrocers, bakers, grocery stores etc

OHPs

vanishing pollutants - CFCs, sprays, diesel cars and lorries
Internet and e-mail to replace fax and postal systems
Reduction is 'generalist/pure education'

Brainstorming session on their ideas of likely changes
Review & Summary
Key points

End 'Thank you for your attention and participation'

67 TUTORIAL QUESTION: TRENDS IN BEHAVIOUR

To: U.R.D. Gaffer
        Managing Director
From: A. Countant
        Marketing Assistant
Date: June 9 2000

The future of Financial Services

In response to your recent query regarding ideas on major developments in the field of consumer behaviour, I would like to submit the following ideas.

(a) I believe that five major changes will be these.

    (i) **Technology.** Advances in communication, computerisation, e-mail and the internet will continue. An increasing number of the population will have access to such media and will result in a significant widening of the range of methods for reaching our potential customers. To this may be added the emergence of additional, non-traditional, outlets for financial services such as telephone and supermarkets.

    (ii) **Political policies.** The recent review of the welfare system has reinforced a growing belief that even a New Labour government cannot afford to support the existing, 'traditional' welfare state. This will mean the emergence of needs for welfare provision which will offer major opportunities for our industry. Linked with this is the changing role of women within our society - becoming breadwinners, following careers, and demanding true equality.

    (iii) **Ageing** population. The demographics are now clear that, with people living longer and birth-rates holding relatively lowly, the emergence of 'Grey Power' as a significant element in the market place is inevitable.

    (iv) **Environmentalism.** The green movement will continue to be influential and will be reinforced by a growing concern with 'ethical' issues.

    (v) **Rising consumer expectations.** The communication revolution has created a sophisticated customer base who are aware of, and concerned with, a much wider range of issues than previously. They are aware of historical scandals such as the mis-selling of private pensions and are increasingly questioning and sceptical. They read newspapers, listen to radio programmes such as 'MoneyBox' and watch consumer programmes on TV. As a result they are becoming fully aware of 'world class standards' - and are now demanding them for themselves.

(b) **Implications for our organisation**

As with any change, each of these developments offer both threats and opportunities to us. Let us take them in turn:

    (i) **Technology,** Here we need to be aware of the new media and develop our marketing systems to take advantage of, for example, the Internet. We should set up a web site and explore the possibility of both informing and selling via this medium. It has an advantage of getting us in touch with what is likely to be an affluent, youngish segment of the population and we can target products such as pensions, PEPs/ISAs, stockmarket services etc. If we can establish early presence we should be well placed to reap significant benefits as the market expands in the future.

    (ii) **Political policies.** The importance, given current government thinking, of private health insurance, sickness insurance, pensions can only increase as we move away from universal benefits and the 'cradle to grave' assumptions of the old Welfare State. There is a huge potential market in these areas and we must position ourselves to be a provider of choice for the expansion in demand that seems bound to come.

(iii) **Ageing population.** In one sense this could be seen as a sub-set of the previous category - but it is so significant that it fully deserves a section of its own. In addition to normal savings and pensions products there is predicted to be a major growth in the demand for insurance to cover residential care for the elderly. Scare stories are already hitting the headlines and this will raise worries in people's minds about whether they will be looked after in their old age. As life expectancy rises and the State welfare provision is diminishing - the potential market would seem to be vast.

(iv) **Environmentalism** is not likely to go away. Ethical issues, in general, may well seem to be an indulgence of the affluent - so it would make sense to develop our portfolio of products to include environmentally green (and/or ethical) products in each category.

(v) **Rising consumer expectations.** This is a function of improved and expanding communication systems and competition. The truism of 'customer as king' remains true and indeed may be becoming inadequate as the notion of 'delighting' the customer becomes the norm. The whole area is a matter of how we are seen by potential customers - reality may not matter as much as perception. The aim, according to Tom Peters, is the 'WOW!!' effect (ie beyond delight). Thus the whole organisation should become geared towards excellence of customer care - we must keep a close eye on our competitors, encourage creativity and originality, and keep ahead.

Financial services has a great future - we must be in the vanguard.

68 TQM AND COMMITMENT

From: H. Elper
To: B. Igcheese
Date: December 8 2000

Commitment to customers and TQM

At yesterday's meeting you mentioned that we must have TQM in place if we are to be serious about our commitment to customers. Having just completed a course which covers both areas, may I put forward the following observations for your consideration.

Commitment to customers may be seen as the basis of success in any competitive market, as a deviation from such a philosophy will allow competitors to erode our market position.

TQM, on the other hand, stems from Japanese organisations and their attempts to make the customer the centre of their operations.

The three basic principles which underpin customer-supplier relationships under TQM are:

(a) The recognition and acceptance of the strategic importance of customers and suppliers - **both internal and external.**

(b) The development of win-win alliances between customers and suppliers rather than exploitative relationships.

(c) The establishment of a supplier-customer relationship based on trust.

These principles are translated into practice by:

(a) Continually collecting information on customer needs, reactions and attitudes.

(b) Feeding back this information throughout the organisation.

(c) Using this information to improve the design, production and delivery of the organisation's product and services.

Customer satisfaction (internal as well as external) is a key objective (indeed, it could be argued that customer satisfaction, in essence, defines quality) and writers such as Tom Peters claim that the aim must be to 'delight' the customer by delivering more than was expected.

In order to be effective, TQM programmes require the following conditions to be fulfilled.

(a) **Total commitment from top management.**

(b) **A definition of customer requirements and obligations via customer care initiatives.**

(c) **Customer orientation as a way of life.** This should therefore stress the importance of departments within organisations regarding each other as internal customers.

(d) **Total staff involvement.** A quality culture must be developed and it is helpful if this pervades the whole organisation as difficulties will arise if one group of staff are trying to improve the quality of what they deliver to customers and are having to deal with other groups who do not see the importance of quality. The need for training in terms of both skills, team working, communication and, particularly, attitudes is very clear.

(e) **Measurement must be continuous and all-embracing.** Required performance needs to be clearly specified in terms which can be measured and mechanisms must be set up which provide clear indicators that these have been achieved. Customer care programmes will require survey data on internal and external customers, on customer behaviour and on the degree to which customer needs are being satisfied.

(f) **Standard processes and procedures to ensure that the output remains consistent.** The monitoring processes provide the basis for learning and consistent improvement.

(g) **Customer objectives** must always be the focus of our attention.

In summary, TQM is a total approach for the organisation which places customers and their care at the very centre of the organisation's activities. It affects internal and external relationships and is not a simple, 'bolt-on', technique.

There are some criticisms of the TQM approach which should be considered, however.

(a) **Sectional interests.** TQM can create 'evangelists' (managers who are seen as fanatical supporters) and this can be divisive within a management team.

(b) **Questionable benefits.** There is a great deal of activity involved in a TQM programme, but it is often difficult to measure and identify benefits other than the award of the ISO 'label'.

(c) **Customers define success.** Not internal processes.

(d) **Recreating the rigid organisation.** Achieving the standard can lead to complacency and a plateauing of effort which can render future change more difficult.

(e) **Lack of evidence.** There is a general lack of satisfactory empirical evidence about the effectiveness of TQM.

(f) **Means vs. ends.** TQM can become an end in itself, particularly when the scheme demands sequential steps and one stage needs to be completed before the next can begin. As a result the real the real purpose of the exercise can be lost.

Conclusion

There is a need to be realistic regarding any TQM initiative. One obvious claim is that such a programme is essential for any organisation which claims to have a customer focus. On the other hand, setting up elaborate systems and expending great energy, effort and money on systems to achieve BS/ISO accreditation can be counter productive, the emphasis on traceability and paperwork diluting any genuine customer focus.

Overall it would appear that we go for a TQM programme but with a clear brief that customer orientation must be maintained.

69   TQM AND CUSTOMER SERVICE

> **Tutorial note.** This is a fairly straightforward question which sets out what is required - all you have to do is provide it!

To: Management Team
From: C. Hampion
Date: December 8 2000

TQM and Competitive Advantage

Introduction

Satisfying our customers has to be our key objective. Customers matter. Customers are the life blood of the organisation. One route to competitive advantage is thought to be via the excellence of our quality and customer care programmes.

I say 'thought to be' because the notion of quality and customer care is essentially a comparative one - it is a function of what our customers expect rather than being measured in absolute terms. There can be instances where the customers may appear to be less crucial. Johns (1994) identifies some possible exceptions.

(a)   We may be competing with other organisations that do not care about their customers either.

(b)   We may be able to compete on factors other than customer care, like price.

(c)   We may not need to compete at all if we are a monopoly.

(d)   We may be a solitary genius, offering products or services which are in great demand and which nobody else is yet in a position to imitate.

The problem with these exceptions is that they are only likely to be temporary conditions if we are operating in a competitive environment.

(a)   In (a) above, all is well until one of the competitors decides to go for a competitive advantage by improving customer service.

(b)   In (b) above, the comfort zone exists on the assumption that price is the sole or dominant factor in the purchasing decision (whether this be organisations or individuals) and, unfortunately for the individual operating under this assumption this is very rarely true. The overwhelming majority of surveys of consumer motivation find that issues such as value for money, quality, availability and service rank higher with the customer than pure price. This is consistent with the 'marketing mix' approach to marketing strategy.

(c) In (c), this scenario may be true in some cases - but the reality in most western economies is that even in the 'traditional' monopolies of the nationalised industries they are being privatised and opened up to competitive pressures.

(d) In (d), the in-demand genius is only of value only so long as the demand for the genius continues.

So it is inescapable that the needs and wants of the consumer must be considered by organisations.

One of the approaches which encompasses this notion is that of Total Quality Management (TQM).

TQM puts the customer centre stage. Satisfying the customer is the fundamental principle of TQM since this approach to business assumes that customers define what is meant by quality.

Juran introduced the concept of managing quality as opposed to just controlling it. He also gave us the definition of quality which is 'fitness for purpose' and placed the responsibility for quality firmly on management.

Basic principles which underpin TQM

(a) The recognition and acceptance of the strategic importance of customers and suppliers - **both internal and external**

(b) The development of win-win alliances between customers and suppliers rather than exploitative relationships

(c) The establishment of a supplier-customer relationship based on trust

These principles are translated into practice by:

(a) Continually collecting information on customer needs, reactions and attitudes.

(b) Feeding back this information widely throughout the organisation.

(c) Using this information to improve the design, production and delivery of the organisation's product and services.

Customer satisfaction (internal as well as external) is a key objective (indeed, it could be argued that customer satisfaction, in essence, defines quality).

Conditions to be fulfilled for TQM programmes to be effective

(a) **Commitment from top management**

The belief must come from the very top and encompass the entire organisation.

(b) **Defining customer requirements and obligations**

Customers (external consumers, employees (internal customers), shareholders, top management, government and so on) can be thought of as a collection of requirements and obligations. Obligations need to be clearly defined and requirements need to be quantified and accepted by both sides as reasonable.

(c) **Customer orientation**

Each internal group in the quality chain comprises a customer and/or supplier to other internal groups.

(d) **Total staff involvement**

A cultural (and sometimes an equivalent structural) change is essential for the achievement of a quality programme. Adopting this philosophy involves a total way of thinking rather than just another technique or fad for management. For this system to work, it is important that all staff are involved and subscribe to the values and attitudes.

(e) **Measurement**

This must be continuous and all-embracing. Required performance needs to be clearly specified in terms which can be measured.

(f) **Standard processes and procedures**

To ensure that the output remains consistent.

(g) **Paying customer objectives**

The end product of any programme must be to satisfy the needs of the paying customer, so all analysis within customer care programmes, and the development of any processes and procedures within such programmes, must relate to those objectives.

Conclusion

TQM is more than a 'bolt-on' management fad. It is a total way of running a business. However, as stated in the introduction, in order for a competitive advantage to accrue, the difference from our competitors must be **noticeable** by our customers - it would be pointless to improve quality continuously and expensively if it is not. If we operate in a market in which all or our competitors have high quality standards we will have little option but to at least match those standards. If we were operating in a purely functional market (such as tickets for the National Lottery) quality may be substantially less significant.

It has been claimed by writers such as Tom Peters that our aim should be to 'delight' the customer by delivering more than was expected. This is sometimes referred to as 'added value', the extra that makes the product/service special. As we achieve ever higher levels of technical and procedural excellence via benchmarking, the 'something special' that the customer perceives is likely to lie in the area of customer care and quality.

TQM holds considerable attractions and advantages for our organisation - but it is not an easy option. If we adopt TQM, the implications for the organisation are set out in the 'principles' and 'conditions' sections above. I believe that it is essential that we follow this path - but even more important is the need for it to be adopted as a total philosophy by all the management and staff. It is a step of great importance - we must consult and debate to gain commitment of staff rather than rushing in with a 'half-baked', imposed programme.

70 DATABASES AND RELATIONSHIP MARKETING

> **Tutorial note.** To answer this question effectively you need to adopt a specific retail sector. We have selected the food and grocery retailing sector which, due to its highly competitive nature, is at the forefront of technology utilisation.

REPORT

To:	Functional managers
From:	R. Holdsworth, Sales and Marketing Manager
Date:	December 8 2000
Subject:	Using IT in customer promotions within the food/grocery sector

BPP PUBLISHING

(a) **Available information technology**

Quantitative data recorded by retailers from shopping scanned through checkouts is now an important source of marketing research information. This is especially so in the highly competitive food and packaged goods sector. The starting point for data capture is the Electronic Point of Sale (EPOS) system.

EPOS data is information captured electronically at the point of sale. Items are scanned, using a bar code reader, by the sales assistant or alternatively scanned by the shopper using a portable reader. Each bar code holds a wealth of information, including item identification, price, store location and so on. Thus, scanning each pack not only registers the sale but updates the data held on the store's computer system. The store's stock account will be updated and the difference between the selling price and cost price recorded to yield profit information on each product. When the stock level falls to a pre-set minimum the EPOS system will trigger a re-order of the item. EPOS data is held on the store's computer facility. Data retrieval can thus yield information specific to a particular store, or to an individual product or area of the country. EPOS data also has a financial value. It can be sold to companies such as Nielsen to assist in the production of retail audits. It can also be sold directly to suppliers. Safeway have recently set up a marketing company - Safeway Information Marketing Company limited (SIMCO) to do just that.

(b) **Increasing sales volumes through effective customer promotions at point of sales**

Data from EPOS systems allows the response to in-store promotions to be measured quickly - at the end of the first week for example. There are numerous other benefits to promotional activities.

(i) Own label coupons can be issued at the checkout to customers who have bought the equivalent branded goods. Catalina coupons link bar codes to loyalty, debit and credit car IDs to assist in profiling customer.

(ii) 'Multi buy' offers can be programmed into the system to make the appropriate deduction on the till receipt. Take up can be assessed and compared to other/previous promotions.

(iii) Special offers and discounted prices can be programmed and initiatives analysed to assess the increase in sales levels.

(iv) Data on margin by product, pack, size, relative sales of own-label and branded products and so on can be used to make decisions on which products should be the focus of new promotions.

(c) **Competitive advantage**

Retailers are now recognising the importance of customer retention - selling more to existing customers is far less costly than finding new customers. Thus building customer loyalty through good relationship marketing is a key objective. An important way of realising competitive advantage is through customer loyalty cards.

The real agenda of loyalty cards, however, is not to win loyalty by rewarding customers. To obtain a card a customer has to give personal details, such as age, marital status, occupation, postcode, and so on. When these personal details are combined with point of sale data on what customers buy, when and how often, database marketing is then made possible. The power of the database can be further enhanced by combining with data from external sources. Linking the postcode to geodemographic databases such as Mosaic (from CCN) and Acorn (from CACI) allows promotions to be targeted at the type of people who are most likely to respond. There are numerous promotional opportunities opened up by utilising the customer database.

(i) Discount coupons sent by post and targeted at customers who buy specific food items.

(ii) Targeting customers who should, but do not buy certain foods, such as meat. Are they vegetarians or do they buy meat in preference from their local butcher?

(iii) Contacting lapsed customers.

(iv) Forming special customer groups to target specific promotions (recipe clubs, customer evenings, and so on).

71 COMPLAINTS PROCEDURES

Consumers who are dissatisfied with a product or service may complain to manufacturers, retailers, service providers and other consumers. Consumer complaint behaviour has been the topic of considerable research and several generalisations have been offered about consumer complaint behaviour.

(1) Those who complain when dissatisfied tend to be members of more upmarket socio-economic groups than those who do not complain.

(2) Personality characteristics, including dogmatism, locus of control, and self-confidence are only weakly related to complaint behaviour, if at all.

(3) The severity of dissatisfaction or problems caused by the dissatisfaction is positively related to complaint behaviour.

(4) The greater the blame for the dissatisfaction placed on someone other than the one dissatisfied, the greater the likelihood of a complaint.

(5) The more positive the perception of retailer responsiveness to consumer complaint, the greater the likelihood of a complaint.

Most people and indeed most companies do not like complaints but actually they are an important source of information for marketers. Complaints inform manufacturers about consumer dissatisfaction and why it occurs, so that the former can do something about the problem. Consumers who are dissatisfied, but do not complain pose a much greater problem, because they will simply refrain from buying the product again, and the manufacturer will have to commission expensive market research to find out about the causes. Some manufacturers therefore try to encourage consumers to complain if they are not satisfied, by providing postage paid return forms or consumer hotlines.

72 ENVIRONMENTAL ISSUES

Environmental issues are of increasing importance to consumers in the UK in a variety of areas. The subject selected for discussion is recycling.

The issue of product disposition and recycling is doubly vital because of its enormous public policy implications. A spokesperson for Powys Council, recently commented that in the 1970s rubbish had cost approximately £5 a tonne to dispose of, in mid 1999 that figure is now £17 and is likely to continue rising. Training consumers to recycle has become a priority in many countries. Japan recycles about 40% of its waste. This relatively high rate of compliance is partly due to the social value the Japanese place on recycling: waste disposal lorries that periodically drive through the streets playing music encourage citizens. Companies continue to search for ways to use resources more efficiently, often at the prompting of activist consumer groups. For example, McDonald's restaurants bowed to pressure by eliminating the use of Styrofoam packages, and its outlets in Europe are experimenting with edible breakfast platters made from maize.

Several studies have examined the relevant goals consumers have to recycle. The most important goals identified were to avoid filling up landfills, waste reduction, re-use materials and save the environment. These were linked to values such as the promotion/avoidance of sickness, achievement of life-sustaining ends and providing for future generations.

Another study reported that the perceived effort involved in recycling was the best predictor of whether people would go through the trouble – this pragmatic dimension outweighed general attitudes towards recycling and the environment in predicting intention to recycle.

Interesting consumer processes occur during lateral cycling, where already purchased objects are sold to others or exchanged for yet other things. Many purchases made are second-hand, rather than new. The re-use of other people's things is making a contribution to the economy. In the UK, car boot sales accounted for some £10 million in 1998 and the antiques market several times that. While traditional marketers have paid little attention to the second-hand market, factors such as concern about the environment, demands for quality and cost and fashion consciousness, are conspiring to make these secondary markets more important.

73   SOCIAL TRENDS

The green consumer of the 1980s has recently been followed, or maybe turned into the concept of the political consumer. The political consumer uses their buying pattern as a weapon against and support for the companies that reflect values similar to the consumer's own. This consumer type selects products according to the company's ethical behaviour, which includes respect for human rights, animal protection, environmental friendliness and support for various benevolent causes.

Companies such as The Body Shop are founded on the idea of natural and non-animal tested products and a maximum of environmental concern. Increasingly, their concerns are being directed towards a broader array of social values. They recently took up the debate of beauty ideals by introducing "Ruby", a Barbie look-alike doll but with considerably rounder forms in order to highlight the thin trend and impossible body ideal of the supermodels also endorsed by Barbie" shape. The strap line was ""there are 3 billion women who don't look like supermodels and only 8 who do". Predictably Mattel Inc., the producers of Barbie, took out an injunction against The Body Shop because they felt that Ruby's face looked too like Barbie's.

Many other companies are now working proactively to avoid the sort of trouble Shell ran into in Europe with the Brent Spar case, or the difficulties French exporters experienced in the wake of nuclear testing in 1996. Organisations are increasingly recognising the political facet of their consumers and are taking action to address their concerns. The mineral water company Ramlosa is campaigning for clean water acts in the developing world together with the Red Cross in Scandinavia under the slogan "Water for Life". British Telecom has run a campaign underlining their work for elderly and disabled people. The two brewery giants Heineken and Carlsberg both withdrew plans for large-scale investments in Burma after consumers' protests against what was seen as direct support for the repressive military government there.

There is a risk that the political consumer may become an even more moralising politically correct consumer, as has occurred in the US's political and cultural climate.

74 NEGLIGENT CONSUMER BEHAVIOUR

Negligent behaviour is composed of those actions and inactions that may negatively affect the long-term quality of life, individuals and society. This type of behaviour can occur in two different contexts. The first form of negligent behaviour occurs due to the consumption of a product that in itself presents a hazard of some sort. The consumption of cigarettes and certain drugs are two examples that fall into this category. A second type of negligent behaviour occurs when the consumer uses a product in an unsafe manner or fail to use safety features and follow safety instructions. Failure to use seatbelts and not following dosage instructions for pharmaceutical products are examples of this form of negligent behaviour.

Two approaches exist to induce people to act in a safer manner. One involves legislation that creates laws forcing consumers to wear seatbelts, bans the advertising and sale of cigarettes and imposes stiffer penalties for drinking and driving. An alternative approach involves the use of marketing techniques to encourage more appropriate consumer actions.

Using concepts derived from behaviour modification theory, one approach might be to reward individuals for demonstrating the desired behaviour. In America, Insurance companies currently use this approach by providing reduced rates to individuals who agree not to drink and drive. Some restaurants give a free meal to the person who agrees not to drink so that they can drive their drinking friends home. The limitation of this approach is that some individuals may refrain from drinking and driving only if they perceive the benefits as outweighing the costs.

75 DELAY MANAGEMENT

Delay in delivery of service is a perennial feature of retailing and other services; indeed it is an inherent liability of a product that is produced and received in an interval of time. Consumers wait for counter service in banks and post offices, for train tickets in booking offices and at the checkout in supermarkets; they also wait for public transport and get delayed in traffic jams. For the individual, delay is frustrating and for the economy it is wasteful as people waiting in line are neither producing not consuming.

Organisations that create delay by poor design of services do so at their peril. Waiting is a punishment that may become associated with the whole service experience and a number of studies have shown that the longer the wait, the lower the evaluation of the whole service. It is likely that people are less bothered by delay when it is expected. This suggests that there are two types of dissatisfaction with delay: a low involvement discontent when the delay is predicted, and a high involvement disconfirmation effect. As delays become more common and impose a more frequent time-cost they also become more predictable. Thus frequency may have off-setting effects on customer toleration of delay; they dislike the greater time cost but find it easier to put up with expected delays.

One study found that people will tolerate a wait better if they have a reason for the delay. The provision of delay information is now standard among transport operators such as airlines, and London Underground provides display boards reporting the wait before train arrivals; such information seems to be much appreciated despite the fact that it does nothing to reduce the waiting time.

People also tend to be less irritated by delay if they can fill their time in some way; one example here is the way in which Disneyland entertains its queues. Research has also suggested that the more control the service provider was thought to have over the delay, the more negative was the perception of the delayed service.

Three approaches to addressing delay management

(a) **Operations management**

Where feasible, management should first try to avoid delays by increasing service supply. For example, supermarket management could count shoppers entering the store and open checkouts in advance of the calculated demand, and they could use their fastest checkout operators at peak times.

(b) **Influence demand**

The second approach uses regulation and incentives to draw demand away from busy periods and towards quiet periods. A reservation system is used for many services and differential pricing may also shift demand

(c) **Perception management**

The last approach is to try to ensure that the customer sees the delay in a way that does least damage. When delay occurs an organisation should seek to offer accurate information. Providing diversion for the queue may also be useful but it is easy to offend customers with mindless music on the telephone.

Often the cause of the delay is accidental or brought about by other service providers eg air traffic controllers, on whom the management has relied. This suggests that the management needs to distinguish between the cause of the delay and responsibility for its consequences. Staff should clearly accept responsibility to remedy a problem, but it will help if they can explain that they did not create it.

76 ELECTRONIC COMMERCE

INTERNAL MEMORANDUM – ELECTRONIC COMMERCE

To: Marketing Department
From: G. Raduate, Marketing Officer
Date: September 6 2000

Introduction

This memorandum has been researched and developed at the request of the marketing department. It will review three key areas: the future of electronic commerce, the implications for our organisation and finally some recommendations. The whole area of electronic commerce is huge and as such I shall endeavour to be concise by using bullet points.

The future of electronic commerce

Electronic commerce is not a distinct marketplace in itself: rather internet technology has created new tools that businesses can use to broaden their markets. Electronic commerce has the potential to bring significant changes. For some it may create opportunities while for others threats. Here are the key aspects:

- Significant differences is usage and attitudes between countries
- At present it is unregulated but this is likely to change
- Information is now viewed as a commodity
- The biggest sellers include PCs, CDs and books
- Can reduce costs and so offer reduced prices

  - Available 24 hours, 7 days a week

The implications for this organisation

These will be dependent on which type of organisation has been selected, for example for travel organisations:

- Gives airlines an opportunity to remove agents and so offer lower prices

- Accurate and up to date schedules and prices need to be available – Virgin were fined for not updating their prices

- Such purchases appeal to more sophisticated and independent travellers

- Allows the more adventurous traveller to 'develop' their own package

- Requires maintenance and monitoring - responsive

Recommendations

For an established organisation such as ours, one of the principal challenges of electronic business is the extent to which its existing value chain is made redundant and whether its competitive advantage is eroded. Various studies have in the past been optimistic about the value and volume of on-line sales. More recent studies have shown that actual usage is growing but not at the exponential rates that had initially been predicted. Rather than asking why should we be involved in electronic commerce we should be asking 'why not?'.

77   DEMANDING / ETHICAL CUSTOMERS

Many organisations have come to realise that customer satisfaction is the only route to long-term sustainable competitive advantage. Equally, customers themselves have begun to flex their muscles, they are much less inclined to accept what they are given and remain silent when they are dissatisfied. They are much more willing to take their business elsewhere when presented with the opportunity to do so and so attracting and retaining loyalty has become a major issue for organisations.

Aspirational

We live and work in a free market economy and as such we have access to more funds and more credit than ever before. The media keeps us informed of the lifestyles of those who are wealthy and famous. We know what they drive, where they go on vacation, what they wear and even what they eat. As such many individuals aspire to have the car of a football star, the dress of an actress, the wallpaper of a minor royal or even the hair style of a sitcom actress. As such it can be said that society is increasingly aspirational, we may not have Jennifer Aniston's fame and fortune but we can have her hairstyle.

The implication for marketing is that these opinion leaders need to be identified so that consumers can copy them. For example Jennifer Aniston is well known for her hairstyle and this was recognised by L'Oreal, the hair product manufacturer. She was selected as their representative with the understanding being that anyone can have her hair by using their products.

Demanding

Research has shown that consumers are more time conscious and so demand more access time, this is one of the key features of electronic commerce. Similarly they are less willing to wait. For example in one organisation, the average time that callers are prepared to wait on hold before they hang up has fallen in two years from 130 seconds to 30 seconds. Customers now expect the person who answers the phone to be able to deal with their request or query immediately rather than be passed around several different departments. They also want more information delivered directly, either by post or through email and they are unlikely to make a second request in the case of a delay. All of these factors have implications for fast, effective and efficient customer services along with realistic and deliverable service policies.

Litigious

While not going so far as to emulate the US tendency to sue for anything and everything, the UK consumer is becoming more sophisticated in terms of their understanding of their rights and their knowledge of the law. This has been reinforced by the increase in consumer related TV and radio programmes. Virgin were recently taken to court and fined for not updating the prices on their web site.

Ethical

In general, ethical issues in terms of how companies behave, have become more important in the last decade. Many companies are now exploiting this new found concern with ethics. The Co-Operative Bank has developed an entire advertising campaign around avoiding investment in countries with oppressive regimes. Ethical issues in marketing can include: failure to inform customers about risks associated with the use of the product, price fixing, tasteful advertising and fair trade.

All of the above factors have clear implications for consumer marketing. Organisations need to be aware of the depth and importance eof these issues and the role they play in consumer decision making.

78 CUSTOMER SATISFACTION AND CUSTOMER DELIGHT

INTERNAL REPORT – FOX LODGE COUNTRY HOTEL

To: B. Ushytail, Head of Marketing
From: C. Ub, Marketing Officer
Re: Customer delight
Date: 6th December 2000

Introduction

The purpose of this report is to explore the key issues of customer satisfaction and customer delight. The report will be divided into three sections. The first part will deal with defining satisfaction and delight while the second will discuss the importance of delight creation. The report will conclude with suggestions as to how customer delight may be achieved.

Satisfaction and delight

Customer satisfaction signifies the fulfilment of basic product/service criteria, i.e. the purchased commodity delivers what it says it will deliver, the packaging and other contributing factors are acceptable, and the price paid is considered to be appropriate. In contrast, delight is a conscious feeling of elation, pleasure, fulfilment and gratification. These feelings arise from the enormous psychological benefits associated with the purchase or the awareness that some special, possibly unique and remarkable degree of service has been addressed.

Delight creation

The term delighters has been coined to explain those features or characteristics which surprise customers positively. They solve a need that the customer did not know could be solved or did not think anyone would solve. Unfortunately, once a delight has been experienced once or twice, the customer begins to increase their expectations, believing that this will be provided permanently. It then becomes an essential ingredient and increases the challenge to delight in other ways.

Delight is likely to lead customers to move from the satisfied category to the very satisfied one. Research has shown that the customer who is merely satisfied is between 7 and 10 times more likely to move to another supplier than a customer who is very satisfied. Thus it is the very satisfied customer who is genuinely loyal and is likely to exhibit repeat behaviour. Furthermore, if the organisation makes a mistake or delivers unusually poor service to this customer, then the customer is likely to overlook this temporary disappointment as they assume it will soon be rectified.

Delight strategies

Any suggested customer service strategies need to be reviewed in the light of a cost benefit analysis. Here are some ideas:

1   A detailed and comprehensive quality related questionnaire. It is standard practice to leave these in rooms but they lack an incentive to complete. The response rate could be improved by incentivising with an opportunity to win a free weekend or more tangibly a room tariff reduction.

2   These results could then be used to determine relative levels of satisfaction for the different services offered. It would be helpful to undertake competitive research, perhaps with a member of staff posing as a customer. These two aspects of research should provide us with a comprehensive overview of our competitive position and the attitude of our current customers. New ideas could include:

3   Different standards of accommodation –at present we offer one standard. As many of customers come here to celebrate a special event, we could offer premium accommodation with appropriate extras e.g. Jacuzzi, champagne, celebration cakes etc.

4   Consider niche weekends for individuals with specific interests e.g. bird watching, cookery, murder mystery etc.

5   Offer loyalty bonuses to regular customers to encourage repeat visits.

6   The above would have to be supported with a thorough customer services training programme. Staff at all levels would need to appreciate the importance of not just customer service but customer delight.

Conclusion

The above report has sought to clarify the issue of customer delight. I trust that you have found its contents useful and look forward to discussing the findings at our next meeting.

79   CUSTOMER 'ISSUES'

Internal memorandum – Sunshine Vacations

To: H.O. Liday, Marketing Manager
From: S. Untan, Marketing Assistant
Re: Recent consumer behaviour research
Date: 6th December 2000

1. Introduction

Recently published research has claimed that customers are swayed by political, ethical, ecological and other 'issue' considerations. The purpose of this memo is to explore the implications this may have for us at Sunshine Vacations. Each of these factors will be considered in turn.

2. Political

Political policies have wide ranging influences, these can include human rights, economic and financial developments as well as legislation. In the context of our organisation we might want to consider any party political affiliations. Some individuals may consider particular countries unattractive due to their political record. It would be our responsibility to review our product policy in this light and ensure that accurate and up to date information is always available.

3. Ethical

The ethical behaviour of organisations has become increasingly important in the past decade. Many companies are now exploiting this new found concern with ethics. The Co-Operative Bank has developed an entire marketing strategy around avoiding investment in for example countries with oppressive regimes or tobacco or arms manufacturers. Ethical issues in marketing can include failure to inform customers about associated risks, price fixing, tasteful communications and the principles of fair trade.

As a travel company we could seek to address these concerns in a variety of ways. For example we can be sure to inform customers of any potential risks if they are travelling to unstable areas and offer appropriate insurance services, should travel not be possible. We might want to review our communications strategy to ensure that our text and photographs do not depict any potentially exploitative situations. Some of our customers may be concerned that we are using local individuals e.g. safari guides and porters on trekking holidays. We need to ensure that these individuals are paid fairly and that our customers know that we are acting responsibly.

4. Ecological

Concern for ecological issues are becoming increasing reported in the media. It has become apparent that natural resources are being depleted and organisations are being told that a large proportion of customers are concerned about the environment and want products that are environmentally friendly. However, this concern is not widespread and it most prevalent amongst the middle classes. As these form the majority of our customer base, we ought to be investigating how we can address their concerns.

Ecological issues could relate to the building of new developments and how these impact on local communities. It may be possible to offer to place customers in low rise, low impact accommodation. Furthermore, transportation issues could be reviewed to ensure energy efficiency.

5. Conclusion

The assumption made at the beginning of this quote is that customers formally acted, as 'rational, economic entities' and this is open to debate. In some selected instances this may still be true but in general, customers have always been driven by their emotions and beliefs. Clear evidence of this has been shown when countries' products have been boycotted as a result of unethical behaviour e.g. South Africa and its former apartheid policy, France and its nuclear testing.

All of the above factors have clear implications for consumer marketing organisations. We need to be aware of the depth and importance of these issues and the role they play in consumer decision making. The implementation of the above suggestions would require the development of sophisticated segmentation to establish customer requirements accurately.

I look forward to discussing these issues with you at our next meeting.

80 MINI-CASE: FAST-FOOD GROUP

PLEASURE FOOD INTERNAL REPORT

To: F. Ries, Marketing Director
From: M. Oveon, Consultant
Date: September 6 2000

Structure of the report

1   Overall aim
2   Background
3   Database acquisition and customer satisfaction
4   Trends in customer segmentation and dynamics
5   Factors affecting overseas expansion
6   Competitive advantage creation
7   Conclusion

1   **Overall aim**

The aim of this report is to offer Pleasure Food guidance regarding the optimal direction that it should pursue in the future. It has been researched and developed at the request of the Marketing Director (UK). Four key areas have been investigated, these are database issues, trends in customers, overseas options and finally the creation of competitive advantage is considered.

2   **Background**

Pleasure Food is a UK based fast food chain that has been operating for over 30 years. Units are located principally in areas of high traffic such as shopping areas, leisure complexes and airports. Some of these units are operated by franchise agreement. The organisation has been growing successfully and now feels that it needs to consider expansion strategies to ensure its future in a highly competitive market.

3   **Database acquisition and customer satisfaction**

Database marketing allows vast amounts of customer data to be stored cheaply and to be used to produce more accurate customer communications as well as other marketing tactics. This is important if Pleasure Food is to gain an advantage over competitors by accessing and applying technologies that a competitor is unable to develop.

When considering database marketing there are two options regarding the database itself. Firstly it could be developed by the organisation in-house. This would necessitate the purchase of appropriate software e.g. Microsoft Access and either the recruitment or training of an individual to develop and maintain the system. The alternative would be to buy an already developed database that would meet requirements. This could be costly and is unlikely to meet all the specified requirements. It could be purchased from one of the major consumer research organisations or other organisations such as charities. The decision regarding the database is likely to be made on the basis of time and cost. If time is of the essence then the best option is to buy in. If there are financial constraints then it is likely to be more cost effective to develop in-house but this will have a longer lead time.

Pleasure Food are interested in securing definitive information about customer satisfaction. Measuring whether customers have got what they wanted can be extremely problematic for a number of reasons.

- Weak anecdotal evidence based on one incidence, especially if such evidence reinforced what people in an organisation want to hear

- Single-incident disasters may be used by one part of the organisation to attack another.

- The views of those customers who complain may be atypical and are not counterbalanced by those who do not.

- Many badly served customers will not complain but will take their business elsewhere.

- The opinions of a small number of highly articulate customers will be given excessive emphasis.

A key element of customer care is finding out what customers want and what they think. Various market research tools can be used to investigate customer satisfaction. However, if surveys for example are to generate authentic data, then questions need to be asked not only about how satisfied customers are with any given element in the service, but also how important that element is to them. If these dimensions of satisfaction and importance are combined, Pleasure Food may then map customer perceptions.

4   **Trends in customer segmentation and dynamics**

Segmentation is the process by which consumers are grouped together according to identifiable characteristics that are relevant to their buying behaviour. The following list highlights those trends that are of relevance to the fast food industry.

- Ageing population
- More people living alone
- Higher standard of living
- Increased leisure time
- Green movement

The changes in population mean that Pleasure Food need to consider what it has to offer the more mature customer as well as the traditional market of teenagers and families. Another change in population is the increase in individuals living alone who may want the convenience of take away food. There is evidence that society is experiencing higher standards of living and increased leisure time both of which provide opportunities for catering establishments. The green movement is particularly strong in the younger market and it may have implications for Pleasure Food's product offering as well as packaging.

Customer dynamics refers to the ways in which consumers interact with organisations. The 1998 Bain report, The Future of Customer Service, makes it clear that customer service demands have increased dramatically over the past five years. According to their results, customers now.

- Demand more access time
- Are less willing to wait
- Demand faster responses
- Want more information
- Have less patience with broken promises
- Complain more

All these factors are relevant to Pleasure Food. They imply longer opening hours, more staff at peak times to ensure faster service, more product information and more feedback opportunities

5   **Factors affecting overseas expansion**

Much research would need to be undertaken before any overseas expansion could be considered. As the organisation has no base overseas it would be wise to engage the services of a professional overseas research organisation. The Department of Trade and Industry should be able to help. Listed below are a number of factors that would need to be considered.

- **Marketing conditions**: differences in retail, distribution and communication systems, promotional regulation/legislation, trade restrictions etc. may affect the potential for research, promotion and distribution in other countries.

- Socio-economic factors: consumers in one country may have different disposable incomes and/or decision-making roles from those in another.

- Segmentation: one country may have different demographic, geographic, socio-cultural and psychological groupings to another.

- Consumption: one country may not use a service or product as much as another or may use it in a different way.

- Needs and wants: the benefits sought from a product in one country may be different in another.

- Language: a promotional theme may not be intelligible or translatable.

6   **Competitive advantage creation**

Competitive advantage comes about as a result of those factors which enable firms to compete successfully on a sustained basis. Michael Porter claims that competitive advantage arises out of the way in which firms organise and perform activities. Pleasure Food can divide its activities into buying, cooking and serving food. There is no reason why customers should not do all these things themselves in their own homes. The customer, however, is prepared to pay for someone else to do all this. The ultimate value a firm creates is measured by the amount customers are willing to pay for its products or services above the cost of carrying out value activities.

Pleasure Food has a number of choices as to how to create this value to develop competitive advantage.

- Become more efficient by serving food faster

- Develop commercial relationships with food manufacturers to obtain the best quality

- Specialise in particular food offerings

- Differentiate with outlets for different types of customer

- Consider overseas opportunities

- Invest in a database to evaluate and improve customer relationships

7   **Conclusion**

This report has covered a wide range of issues that will impact on the future success of Pleasure Food. The marketplace is competitive and challenging. Nonetheless I feel confident that the consideration and implementation of the above proposals will ensure the continued success of Pleasure Food. I look forward to presenting these findings to the Board.

81   MINI-CASE: PRINTING COMPANY

EXECUTIVE REPORT

To: John Rush, Managing Director, Platinum Print
From: Raymond Faulkner, Marketing Services
Re: Recent meeting
Date: 6th December 2000

1. **Introduction**

    At our last meeting, concern was expressed regarding the future of Platinum Print and in particular four issues were raised. The purpose of this report is to present the findings of my investigations into these key issues.

2   **Customer feedback approaches**

    Customer feedback is an essential aspect of management information and is a valuable source of market research. A variety of informal and formal methods can be used to obtain such information:

    •   Surveys and questionnaires – either by post or administered in person by the sales representative, useful for gathering quantitative data but often a low response rate

    •   Anecdotal evidence from contact staff – informal verbal discussions may be a useful source but need to be accurately recorded

    •   Focus groups – to provide, insightful, qualitative data, useful in the early stages of research to get a feel for the subject matter

    •   Interviews – another qualitative method but usually on a one-to-one basis, need to ensure that the chosen sample is representative

    •   Complaints management – ensure that a proper complaints procedure is in place and regard it as a data gathering opportunity

    •   Suggestion schemes – offering incentives for realistic ideas regarding efficiency or effectiveness improvement

    Given Platinum Print's relatively small customer base it would seem appropriate to use a qualitative approach, a series of interviews or small focus groups would be feasible. The end user and other direct customers could be assessed using an incentivised questionnaire to encourage response.

3   **Relationship marketing**

    Relationship marketing can be defined as the successor to mass marketing and is the process by which information about the customer is consistently applied by the company when developing and delivering products or services. Such developments can be communicated to the customer in a number of ways. For example via specially targeted promotions and product launches. The objective of such activities is to build long term relationships by offering individual attention.

    The justification for relationship marketing comes from the needs to retain customers. There are five different levels of relationship:

    •   Basic – selling with no further contact

    •   Reactive – customer is encouraged to call salesperson

    •   Accountable – salesperson asks customer for feedback

    •   Proactive – salesperson contacts customer on a regular basis

- Partnership – salesperson and customer work together to ensure mutual satisfaction

In the case of Platinum Print, it would appear that you have stopped at the reactive stage. In order to implement a more relationship based approach, I would recommend that you encourage salespeople to move onto the following two stages. Either verbal or written surveys could be undertaken to establish consumer satisfaction and requirements. Accurate and detailed sales records should be kept to ensure that regular customer contact is maintained. Technology is likely to be the key factor here. Software developments have made databases flexible and powerful enough to hold large amounts of customer specific data and this option should be investigated.

4 Customer focused employees

Customer care programmes are devoted to maximising the benefits a customer receives within the operating constraints of the business. This means that the operations staff who deliver the service should do so with a marketing philosophy in mind. A variety of activities could be adopted to encourage a more customer service based approach. These include:

- The development of reward and recognition schemes based on customer-service performance levels e.g. employee of the month

- Role-modelling customer focus from the top of the company e.g. senior management being seen to be customer active

- The use of customer-centric teams to ensure consistent satisfaction and quality

- Customer visits – not just from the sales representatives but by those who will be undertaking the work so that needs are understood

- Recruitment of customer-friendly employees with effective inter-personal skills

- Internal publicity regarding the benefits of a customer focus, both with regards to internal and external customers

5 Competitive advantage

Competitive advantage comes about as a result of those factors that enable firms to compete successfully on a sustained basis. Porter claims that competitive advantage arises out of the way in which firms organise and perform activities. Activities are the means by which a firm creates value in its products. Activities incur costs and, in combination with other activities, provide a product or service that earns revenue. Platinum Print's activities can be divided into purchasing raw materials, printing mass and bespoke stationery and selling it to customers. There is no reason, in theory, why customers with limited information technology skills could not do this themselves. The customer is prepared to pay for Platinum Print to do this for them. The ultimate value Platinum Print creates is measured by the amount customers are willing to pay for its products or services above the cost of carrying out value activities.

Platinum Print has a number of choices as to how to create competitive advantage:

- Superior customer service e.g. ensure 100% delivery in 48 hours

- The creation of new customer segments, thus attacking different marketplaces

- The development of total customer solutions, this could involve Internet web site design, mail order processing through label printing etc.

6 Conclusion

The above report has sought to address the key concerns expressed at our meeting last week.

The concept of effective customer feedback is a crucial one for the organisation. A variety of methods have been discussed and organisation specific recommendations made.

The concept of relationship marketing appears to have considerable relevance for Platinum Print's transactions with stationery supply companies and other direct customers, provided that the returns justify the effort.

The implementation of a customer care programme should be encouraged with active participation from all employees. A set of tactical examples has been provided.

The issue of competitive advantage has been discussed and a few suggestions made. It is likely that this list could be substantially extended after customer and employee consultation.

I hope that you have found this report's contents useful and look forward to our meeting next week.

Test your knowledge

1   What are the criteria by which models of consumer behaviour are evaluated?

2   What is the difference between a customer and a user?

3   Why do customers have to make choices?

4   Who are your 'internal customers'?

5   Does qualitative data come from

(a) narrative, descriptive evidence, or
(b) numbers?

6   Why do we need to identify the customer?

7   List the internal factors affecting perception.

8   What is the difference between a 'laboratory' experiment and a 'field' experiment?

9   What sort of research involves in-depth interviews and focus groups?

10   What are the product characteristics that influence adoption?

11   Identify three types of segmentation approach.

12   What do we mean by the 'affective component of attitudes'?

13   What are the qualities that make a segment useful?

14   What do we call it when we refer to something which we believe has been perceived sub-consciously?

15   List the six stages of marketing research.

16   What do we call the study of population characteristics such as age, gender, occupation etc.?

17   Why do you need to be careful when dealing with secondary data?

18   Psychographic segmentation is sometimes said to be AIO analysis - what do A, I and O stand for?

19   List the external factors influencing attention and perception.

20   What is data?

21   Name three sources of secondary data.

22   List four types of questionnaire.

23   We have a number of different types of survey - how do we classify them?

24   What do we call the type of question used to categorise a respondent in a survey?

25   Why are families important to an understanding of consumer behaviour?

26   Is there any evidence to support the notion that subliminal perception works?

27   List the stages of the decision-making process.

28   By what names are secondary and primary research also known?

29   What is an omnibus survey?

30   Give two examples of types of syndicated research.

31   In qualitative research people are interviewed individually or in groups. What are the correct terms for such interviews?

32   What is the difference between market research and marketing research?

33   What sources of error are there in marketing research?

34   In questionnaire design, questions relating to classification data should always come at the beginning of the questionnaire. True or false?

35   When conducting research using a structured questionnaire, what are the three key ways of administering the questionnaire?

36   What is wrong with using such words as sometimes, regularly, and dinnertime in a questionnaire?

37   Explain what is meant by the term compensatory decision rules.

38   What characteristics define early adopters?

39   What are the key differences between limited and extended problem solving?

40   **What is social marketing?**

1   (a) Validity
    (b) Factual accuracy
    (c) Rationality
    (d) Completeness
    (e) Simplicity
    (f) Originality
    (g) Heuristic power
    (h) Explanatory power
    (i) Predictive power

2   A customer pays for the product or service while the user uses it, but may not pay for it.

3   Because their resources are limited.

4   Other departments and staff within the organisation.

5   (a)

6   In order to identify their needs for products and services and to identify the marketing mix required to satisfy those needs.

7   Motivation, interest, expectations.

8   Laboratory experiments are 'artificial' and field experiments are 'real world'.

9   Qualitative

10 (a) Relative advantage
    (b) Compatibility
    (c) Complexity
    (d) Trialability
    (e) Observabillity

11 Life stage; life style; socio-demographic (class/status)

12 The emotional element

13 (a) Measurable
    (b) Accessible
    (c) Substantial
    (d) Relatively stable

14 Subliminal perception

15 (a) Problem diagnosis
    (b) Clarification of options
    (c) Research design
    (d) Data collection
    (e) Data analysis
    (f) Report presentation

16 Demographics

17 It may have been collected for different reasons or it may be out of date

18 Attitudes, interests, opinions

19 (a) Intensity of the stimulus
    (b) Contrast
    (c) Novelty
    (d) Position
    (e) Repetition

BPP PUBLISHING

20   Unprocessed information

21   Governmental sources, non-governmental sources, marketing research organisations

22   Structured, unstructured, self-completed, interviewer completed

23   They are classified according to the location of the interviews.

24   Classification

25   They are consuming, decision making and socialising units

26   No

27   (a) Problem recognition
          (b) Information search
          (c) Evaluation of alternatives
          (d) Decision
          (e) Post purchase evaluation

28   Desk and field research

29   This is a shared survey where the research design is constant and usually regular, but the questions vary according to what the clients wish to ask. They effectively 'jump on' to the omnibus as it comes along and pay for whatever they require.

30   Panel research (consumer/household or business) and retail audits

31   Depth interviews and focus groups

32   Market research seeks to discover if there is a market for a product or service and is therefore narrower than marketing research. Marketing research looks at the elements of the marketing mix and therefore focuses on pricing, distribution and promotional issues as well as deciding what the product should be, how it should be packaged etc.

33   Potential errors are numerous and include research design, incorrect data collection methods used, non-response, sampling error, inappropriate questionnaire wording, answers written down wrongly, data entered onto computer wrongly, misinterpretation of results (amongst others)

34   False. They should come at the end except where a quota needs to be filled and then it is permissible to put such questions at the beginning to eliminate people outside the quota.

35   Face-to-face interviewing (at home/office or in the street), telephone interviewing and self-administered (including postal questionnaires and those put in magazines, hotel rooms and on restaurant tables).

36   They are ambiguous.

37   Compensatory decision rules allow information, about attributes of competing products to be averaged, poor standing on one attribute may be offset by positive standing on another.

38   Early adopters are people who are receptive to new styles because they are involved in the product category and place high value on being fashionable.

39   Limited problem solving is a process in which consumers are not motivated to search for information or rigorously evaluate each alternative; instead they use simple decision rules to arrive at a purchase decision. Extended problem solving is an elaborate decision-making process often initiated by a motive that is central to the self-concept and accompanied by perceived risk. The consumer tried to collect as much information as possible and carefully weighs product alternatives.

40   Social marketing is the promotion of causes and ideas, such as energy conservation, charities and population control.

Advanced Certificate in Marketing

Test Paper: June 2000 examination

8.35 The Marketing Customer Interface

3 Hours Duration

This examination is in two sections.

Part A is compulsory and worth 40% of total marks.

Part B has **SIX** questions, select **THREE**. Each answer will be worth 20% of the total marks.

DO NOT repeat the question in your answer but show clearly the number of the question attempted.

Rough workings should be included and ruled through after use.

DO NOT OPEN THIS PAPER UNTIL YOU ARE READY TO START UNDER EXAMINATION CONDITIONS

Part A

The Walters Chemical Company

Cleaning and rust preventative chemicals compounds are the major products of the Walters Chemical Company, which has over 2000 different formulations to meet all the expectations demanded by its customers (engineering companies and car manufacturers).

Frequently, a Walter Sales Representative will be called in by a customer to resolve technical problems being experienced with the application of one of the Walters compounds. Although well-trained, the Sales Representative commonly does not know the answer and telephones his Head Office for professional help. Calls of this nature are referred to the Technical Services Department.

Normally the trouble must be resolved within hours, if possible, in order to keep production moving in the customer's factory. Quick and responsive service is therefore important. Sometimes the Technical Services Department can give immediate help but more commonly it has to investigate further, thus necessitating a delay coupled with a promise to phone back once it is in a position to offer well-informed advice.

The Sales Representatives often complain that Technical Services do not fulfil their telephone promises. Follow-up calls from the Representative lead to statements by Technical Services that there is no record of the previous request, or that additional information to be supplied by the customer has not yet been received, or that the problem is being worked on without the solution having yet been found.

The Technical Services Manager has devised a three-copy form which each Sales Representative is supposed to complete whenever they have a customer problem requiring specialised assistance. However, he claims that the Representatives do not use the form if they can avoid it: "They would rather telephone, tell you about the problem and, if there is any trouble later, deny that they didn't supply you with all the facts. They then blame Technical Services for not doing its job. And every sales representative seems to think that his requests are the only ones the matters."

The Sales Representative, for their part, believe that they do give complete information to Technical Services, but that the department only hears what it wants to hear. The view of the Sales Representative is that 'Filling out forms is fine for possible new customers, but for existing customers who run into trouble, we have to know the answer straight away. And Technical Services must have a poor filing system: they can never find any evidence of our previous calls. The only way to get them to do anything is shout and make a nuisance of yourself.'

Part A

Question 1

Your answer should be written in the form of a report to the Chief Executive of the Walters Chemical Company. It is permissible to make assumptions by adding to the case details given above, provided that the essence of the case study is neither changed nor undermined in anyway by what is added.

(a) It appears that there is considerable hostility between the Sales function and the Technical Services Department. Suggest causes for the conflict and propose appropriate remedies.

(10 marks)

140

(b) The interdepartmental conflict seems to be one factor which prevents the people in Technical Services from being sufficiently customer focused. What can be done to promote more customer-facing attitudes and behaviour amongst this group? **(10 marks)**

(c) The communication process between the Walters Chemical Company and its customers are neither efficient nor effective. How could they be improved? **(10 marks)**

(d) So far the company has not created or applied any mechanism for systematically soliciting customer feedback. Outline and justify the methods which you think they should use.

(10 marks)
(40 marks in total)

Part B – Answer THREE questions only

Question 2

It is predicted that in the future, for most societies there will be many more older people in proportion to other population categories. Assuming this prediction to be accurate, indicate what you would say if you were to speak at a Marketing Conference on the following issues:

(a) What are the factors contributing to this trend?

(b) In what ways can older people be usefully segmented.

(c) What marketing opportunities are represented by growing numbers of older people?**(20 marks)**

Question 3

Your immediate Senior Marketing Manager, working for a large newspaper, has begun to express alarm about the effects of electronic commerce on the business. Write a report for her in which you examine the likely impact:

(a) For the newspaper.

(b) For the world of business as a whole. **(20 marks)**

Question 4

How can customer service be used to create a genuinely sustainable competitive advantage? Illustrate your answer with relevant examples. **(20 marks)**

Question 5

Answer only **ONE** of the following.

Outline and justify a marketing research plan for:

Either

(a) A fashion conscious clothing manufacturer that wants to find out which new designs will be most appealing to college students. **(20 marks)**

OR

(b) A cigarette firm which wants to gain some insights into attitudes towards smoking among teenagers and young adults. **(20 marks)**

Question 6

Sometimes companies move from healthy profitability to substantial profit erosion or even losses because, it is claimed, they have lost touch with their customers. Using recent examples in order to illustrate your argument, explain why organisations make mistakes of this kind, and show how they can be avoided. **(20 marks)**

Question 7

As the Marketing Manager for a soft drinks company, write a report for your Director in which you address the following issues:

(a) The factors which your company should take into account when deciding which market segments to address and which ones to leave alone.

(b) The processes which can lead to the discovery of new and potentially profitable segments.

(c) The ways in which sales from existing segments may be developed incrementally.

(20 marks)

Suggested answers

DO NOT TURN THIS PAGE UNTIL YOU
HAVE COMPLETED THE TEST PAPER

1   CONFIDENTIAL INTERNAL REPORT

To: C. Ompound, Chief Executive
From: C. Atalyst, Marketing Assistant
Date: 12th June 2000
Ref: Sales and Technical Services Relations

Introduction

This report has been researched and written at the request of the Sales and Technical Services (TS) divisions. It appears that communications difficulties are arising at various points with in the organisation and the objective of this report is to analyse these and offer suggestions as to how they may be resolved.

Conflict and potential remedies

At present customers contact their sales representative with their technical problems. The representative then visits the customer and commonly does not know the answer and so contacts the TS division. Sales complain that TS do not keep their promises or act quickly enough and TS claim that Sales do not provide sufficient information, if at all and that the problem is a complex one that needs more time.

This pattern of behaviour would indicate a certain level of stereotyping – sales are all talk (often related to bonus schemes) and have no technical knowledge, TS are not customer focused and think they are superior. This behaviour is reinforced in a group situation and very often limited direct contact with the other party. This is likely to be fuelled by selective perception where effective communication and problem resolution is ignored but conflicting situations are exaggerated.

A number of options could be considered to seek to minimise this conflict. These include: the creation of joint-problem solving or performance-improvement teams; inter-group rotational assignments so that the two teams not only get to know each other better and so understand their responsibilities but also to improve customer contact; exercises in which the groups explicitly share their perceptions of each other (often this is done as part of an away day, off site with some team building activities). Other options include training to share skills and the consideration of role modelling from the senior management of each function.

Customer care and Technical Services

There is evidence to suggest that this interdepartmental conflict is only one factor that prevents the TS team from being sufficiently customer focused. As such, consideration needs to be given to promoting more customer-facing attitudes and behaviour amongst this group. Such a strategy could include account management with deliberate interaction and visits involving customer locations. Reward and recognition processes could be adopted to help motivate TS staff and improve performance. At a more basic level consideration needs to be given to customer awareness at the recruitment level so that technical staff not only have technical skills but can also interact with customers (with support from the training function). Customers should be encouraged to provide direct feedback to TS, irrespective of whether their comments are positive or negative. This should result in TS having more customer ownership and responsibility.

Customer communication

It would appear that the communication processes between the organisation and our customers are neither efficient nor effective and this is an important problem that needs to be addressed. It may be that customers are unsure of whom to contact and as such it may be appropriate to set up a problem solving hotline to names client managers with TS. Other forms of contact apart from writing and telephoning could be considered, such as direct email contact. If this were to be considered it is important that a named individual check this on a regular basis to ensure effective communication. Many technical based organisations offer a list of FAQs (Frequently Asked Questions) in an attempt to reduce customer contact and increase customer added value. This could either be in leaflet or Internet site format. This approach has been adopted by companies such as IBM who found that the creation and maintenance of FAQ pages on their website resulted in a significant reduction in fault calls and so saved millions of dollars.

It is important that all three parties (sales, TS and the customer) are fully aware of how problems are being progressed and the merger of the two divisions would facilitate this so that only one record with open access would be maintained.

Customer feedback mechanisms

There are really two feedback issues here, firstly how we get feedback on our performance to date and secondly how continuous feedback is obtained in the future. Options such as postal/telephone/email surveys could be considered. These could be incentivised to encourage a positive response rate. One to one interviews (to be conducted by someone not involved with either department) could be considered but given our substantial customer base these are likely to be costly and time consuming. Another alternative would be focus groups were customers are brought together to discuss their experiences. Again the issue of incentivisation would need to be considered to encourage a valid response.

In the interest of speed it is recommended that an initial incentivised survey is conducted and that this is then followed up with regular focus groups.

Conclusion

It is apparent that the situation described above is no longer acceptable as it is likely to impact not only on our profits but also on our reputation. I look forward to discussing the contents of this report with you at our next meeting.

2   **Notes for the June 2000 UK Marketing Conference**

Introduction

Greet the audience and introduce self.

Explain that the focus of this presentation will be the predicted growth of the folder person segment.

Three key areas will be discussed: factors contributing to this trend; segmentation strategies for this market and finally an evaluation of potential marketing opportunities.

Contributing factors

A combination of factors have contributed to the steady increase in the over 55s segment. Government statistics indicate that the UK life expectancy is increasing due to medical intervention and a better understanding of health care issues. Birth rates are also in steady decline with women deciding to have smaller families, leave child rearing to later in their careers or indeed not to have children. Some individuals in the over 55 segment are now realising their aspiration to retire early and live on their private or company pensions and it is believed that this contributes to longevity.

Segmentation strategies

A number of different variables may be used when considering how this market can be segmented. These include geographic location (for example certain coastal areas in the UK may attract this segment due to the climate and services available); socio-economic status and income levels (working v non-working and private/company pension v state pension); family life cycle (responsibility for children); lifestyle (for example active v non-active).

It is recognised that many professional individuals retire from salaried employment early but then undertake consultancy work on a freelance basis. This is particularly the case in education and local government. As such these individuals may be particularly appropriate for email/Internet communication.

Marketing opportunities

The segmentation discussion indicates the diversity apparent in this age category. A significant range of marketing opportunities exist, here are just a few:

Personal finance: insurance, pensions, trust funds, investments, releasing capital from property, private medical care

Leisure: travel, fitness equipment, child free hotels/resorts, book clubs and magazine subscriptions, short courses

Food and drink   health supplements and foods, off peak discounts in restaurants, fine wines

Conclusion

I do hope that you have found this presentation useful. Government statistics clearly indicate that the over 55s are a large and growing segment and as such must be recognised and targeted. Thank you for your attention and I will now be happy to take questions from the floor.

3   **Marketing report**

To: Janet Streetreporter, Senior Marketing Manager
From: James Sniffitout, Marketing Assistant
Date: 12th June 2000
Ref: Electronic commerce and the newspaper industry

At yesterdays marketing meeting, you expressed some concern regarding the effects of electronic commerce on our business. Please find below a preliminary report on this issue.

Overview

E-commerce is the topic of the moment and it is almost impossible to read a newspaper or magazine or listen to a TV or radio broadcast without it being mentioned. Much is made of the problems being experienced by certain dotcom companies while limited reference is made to those who are successful. What cannot be is disputed is that more and more individuals are going on-line either at work or home or both and this increase looks likely to continue. One of the key advantages of the Internet that should concern us is the speed at which information can be accessed at a relatively low cost

E-commerce and the newspaper industry

Our newspaper focuses on UK and European news items with the emphasis on political and business analysis. As such our core advantage is our journalists who have years of experience and considerable contacts in their own field. This advantage is difficult to replicate. Our research supports these comments.

Those organisations who operate news based web sites are providing a service to those who want updated news fast, perhaps while away from home and so unable to access other media. Many offer a customised service where for example they can ask for information on particular countries or companies. This is now replacing the way in which readers scan newspapers for those subjects that interest them, while filtering out those that do not. This customisation strategy is being replicated in a variety of different industries including book and clothes selling. Some dotcom companies consider this to be a premium service and charge accordingly. This may be an opportunity we wish to investigate.

Another facility offered by other information based companies is the ability to search through back copies. For example, if an individual was considering a share purchase, they could review the news regarding the company in question for the past quarter to help their decision making. This would be most time consuming to replicate in a print environment.

It is likely that e-commerce will have an impact on sales but it is worth remembering that a small but significant proportion of the population still like to read their news in print. As such the challenge for us is to provide those readers with added value to secure their future custom. At the same time we need to provide a news service to those who prefer to access their news via the Internet and again provide additional value added services.

E-commerce and business

One of the most significant changes that e-commerce is encouraging is the elimination of intermediaries unless they can find some way of adding value. For example, the majority of individuals purchasing books tend to know what they want, as they will be buying because of recommendation or review. As such the level of personal contact required is limited. A number of Internet based organisations have entered this market and captured a relatively high proportion of market share through offering a very wide range of books at lower than retail outlet prices.

As this is an emerging communication and distribution mechanism, many organisations are learning as they develop the systems and procedures to manage this form of commerce. The press indicates that many have been unsuccessful as they have failed to understand the marketplace, the technology and the costs involved.

Conclusion

As you can see from the above brief report, this is a significant subject and one that needs further detailed investigation before any action is taken. Despite the hype regarding e-commerce and the stories of organisations that have been unsuccessful, there is no doubt that the information industry is one that will be severely affected by this form of communication. As such it is one that we cannot ignore if we are to remain competitive. If we decide to go along this path then we will either have to recruit skilled and experienced individuals or outsource. I look forward to discussing the contents of this report with you at our next meeting.

4   As markets become increasingly saturated and it becomes easier to replicate manufactured products, organisations are recognising that customer service is an essential means for differentiation and reputation enhancement. It is recognised by leading business writers that when organisations seek to develop genuinely sustainable competitive advantage through their customer service offering, that they can only succeed if the service aspect of the business is integrated with the internal service ethos.

Even within the context of customer service much can be replicated. For example 24 hour helplines, return guarantees and delivery promises are now offered as standard by many organisations. The challenge is to develop aspects of customer service first so that when they are replicated, customers still remember the organisation who was first. Marks and Spencer were one of the first high street stores to offer a refund policy and though this has been copied by many others, it still forms part of their quality related image.

Access to the right person at the right time is an important issue when dealing with complaints and this has been taken on board by the car repair organisation Kwik Fit. If customers have a problem with a service provided by this organisation they can have direct access to the Chief Executive Officer. It is unlikely that this service is used on a regular basis but it is a visible and unusual part of their customer service strategy.

Other ways in which an organisation can turn their customer service offer into something which cannot be copied include the extensive use of personalised service (many up market department stores offer personal shoppers to save time for their more exclusive clients); compulsory reliance on components from the original supplier (as used by General Electric); the creation of specific promises which competitors cannot match because they lack coverage, resources or economies of scale (one of the larger DIY chains promises that if a product can be found elsewhere for less, then they will pay 10% of the cost price).

Customer service and more importantly the perception of customer service levels is becoming increasing important in both business to business and consumer consumption. An example of the importance surrounding customer focus is the battle between the two UK supermarket companies, Sainsbury and Tesco. Tesco comfortably beat Sainsbury on loyalty, satisfaction, trust and awareness, according to independent research conducted by MORI in 1997.

5   **Marketing Research Plan for Withit Ltd**

Objective

The purpose of this marketing research plan is to provide Withit's management team with some ideas as to how they can gain an understanding of how college students view their new designs.

Type of research

Essentially there are two types of research; quantitative tends to deal with facts e.g. how much do you spend on clothes per month and so results in statistics. Qualitative tends to deal with more abstract concepts, for example attitudes, opinions and beliefs e.g. do you think that this design is fashionable. This type of research does not tend to generate statistics but rather indicates a depth of feeling. In this instance Withit are seeking to determine attitudes and as such a predominantly qualitative approach is recommended.

When undertaking research, organisations have two choices, either find (and often pay for) research that another person or organisation has conducted, this is known as secondary research, or they can generate new research and this is known as primary. Many research projects include both options and use secondary research to help determine the format of the primary to avoid needless and often expensive repetition.

The fashion market is highly competitive and very fast moving. As such the quantity and quality of secondary research is likely to be limited. It would be worthwhile monitoring the fashion and style press as these are used by the target market as reference material but it will be necessary to undertake primary research to fulfil Withit's objective.

Sample

Appropriate sampling is essential in research to determine validity and reliability. Clearly not all those who may purchase this type of clothing can be researched, if this were the case they would be known as a universal sample. Rather, a representative proportion needs to be researched. This will not only save money but if the selected sample is truly representative, then the research is likely to produce almost identical results to a universal sample.

In this instance the key sampling variables are likely to be age, gender and level of disposable income. When selecting samples there are a number of options available. A random sample could be used where say every tenth person who fits the criteria and passes a certain location is asked to participate. A quota sample can be used where the details of the universal sample are known. For example, if within a given region, it is known that 60% of the under 25 market are female, then this should be replicated in the chosen sample.

I would recommend that a quota sample be undertaken. This will highlight any differences in the aforementioned variables and so allow Withit to develop a more detailed understanding of the variation within their target market.

Methods

A wide variety of research methods are available. These include survey, individual and group interviews, experimentation and observation. In most research projects, a combination approach is adopted to provide a balanced view. If access were available to lists of consumers who fit the variable requirements, then direct contact could be made by phone or letter. Withit could consider becoming involved with a fashion based web site and using that as a platform to gather information. Street surveys could take place and to add depth to their findings, respondent details could be taken and these then followed up with interviews.

My recommendation would be to adopt a combination approach using street interviews with both quantitative and qualitative questions (perhaps showing photos of designs) and then following these up with group interviews to add qualitative depth.

Conclusion

I hope that you find this draft marketing research plan interesting. I have suggested a combination research approach using quota samples to provide validity assurance. I look forward to discussing my suggestions with you at our next meeting.

6   In recent years a number of formerly very profitable and reputable organisations have lost market share, in part because they appear to have lost touch with their customers. Two examples will now be discussed to illustrate this point, IBM and Marks and Spencer.

IBM is a huge US based information technology organisation. They have a global presence and a reputation for success and innovation. This has been tainted in recent years as they have failed to demonstrate their ability to be competitive and marketing focused. Here are some indications of this:

- Complacent attitude that the future will resemble the past and that consumers' needs and wants are unlikely to change significantly

- Supreme confidence in their own superiority based on their long period of success. This meant that they did not need to try so hard as consumers had limited choice

- Remoteness from the marketplace and lack of competitive and consumer awareness

- A reward system for the salesforce which encouraged the selling of large systems which were not always appropriate. In certain instances this resulted in negative publicity

- An inward-looking and bureaucratic structure which failed to encourage internal and external communication

- The pursuit of a sales mentality rather than a marketing orientation

Marks and Spencer has a reputation in the UK for quality food and clothing. In recent years it has sought to move outside the UK and this has had varying degrees of success. The past two years have proved difficult for them, as they have seen their sales and profits steadily decrease. Here are some suggestions as to why this may have happened:

- As with IBM, a certain degree of complacency and misplaced confidence, having been in a comfortable position in the market for so long

- Problems within the boardroom have been well publicised and this has resulted in a lack of management confidence

- Certain lines have been particularly slow to move and this has resulted in early seasonal sales thus affecting profits and reputation

- These buying problems indicate a lack of understanding regarding what their customer base want

A number of lessons can be drawn from these two examples. There is a need for two way communication between the organisation and the customer base to ensure that the organisation stays close to the customer. Organisations need to be aware of changes in customer tastes and levels of disposable income so they can respond appropriately. All organisations need to be relentless in the pursuit of innovation. Marks and Spencer for example, in co-operation with manufacturers, are developing new fabrics and new food products to meet increasingly demanding customers. Finally, a programme of intensive competitive monitoring is required by all organisations to understand what is happening in the marketplace and to help identify opportunity gaps.

7   Fizzy Marketing Report

To: C.Ola, Marketing Director
From: B.Ubbles, Marketing Manager
Date: 12th June 2000
Ref: Recent marketing meeting

Introduction

At our last marketing meeting a number of segmentation issues were raised which you asked me to report back on. This report will focus on segmentation factors, processes and development.

Segmentation factors

Segmentation is an essential aspect of marketing. There are three requirements for effective market segmentation. The first is that the segment must be measurable that is it must be possible to acquire or obtain information about that segment. Secondly the segment must be accessible so that the organisation can focus effectively on the chosen segment using marketing methods. Finally, the segment must be substantial so that it is large enough to be worth considering for separate marketing cultivation.

In order to develop useful segments it is essential that the following are considered: the potential segment profitability; trends in segment style, preferences etc; compatibility of the segment with the organisation's mission and objectives; availability of methods through which the segment may be precisely targeted.

Segmentation processes

The discovery of new and potentially profitable segments can arise via a variety of mechanisms. Internal communication, especially from those in the sales function should be encouraged as they are in daily contact with distributors who in turn are in daily contact with customers. Creative thinking within the organisation should be positively encouraged as not only is this likely to generate ideas but will also provide the workforce with a sense of contribution and ownership. Meticulous monitoring and observation of relevant social trends is essential e.g. the need for energy drinks to help people stay awake, the interest in natural products with purported chemical properties etc.

Existing segment development

Several existing and profitable segments have been identified and we should look to develop these. Ways in which this could be achieved include new product development; brand extensions perhaps through offering existing products in different sizes; added value service enhancements such as rewards for bulk purchase or the opportunity to buy special merchandise; and finally opportunities to appeal to other individuals or groups within current segments, for example other family members.

Conclusion

This report has sought to outline important segmentation issues for Fizzy. I believe that a number of opportunities exist in this area and I look forward to discussing these with you at our next meeting.

Topic Index

BPP PUBLISHING

CIM Order

To BPP Publishing Ltd, Aldine Place, London W12 8AA

Tel: 020 8740 2211. Fax: 020 8740 1184

Mr/Mrs/Ms (Full name) _____

Daytime delivery address _____

Postcode _____

Daytime Tel _____   Date of exam (month/year) _____

	5/00 Texts	9/00 Kits	Tapes
CERTIFICATE			
1 Marketing Environment	£17.95 ☐	£8.95 ☐	£12.95 ☐
2 Customer Communications in Marketing	£17.95 ☐	£8.95 ☐	£12.95 ☐
3 Marketing in Practice	£17.95 ☐	£8.95 ☐	£12.95 ☐
4 Marketing Fundamentals	£17.95 ☐	£8.95 ☐	£12.95 ☐
ADVANCED CERTIFICATE			
5 The Marketing Customer Interface	£17.95 ☐	£8.95 ☐	£12.95 ☐
6 Management Information for Marketing Decisions	£17.95 ☐	£8.95 ☐	£12.95 ☐
7 Effective Management for Marketing	£17.95 ☐	£8.95 ☐	£12.95 ☐
8 Marketing Operations	£17.95 ☐	£8.95 ☐	£12.95 ☐
DIPLOMA			
9 Integrated Marketing Communications	£17.95 ☐	£8.95 ☐	£12.95 ☐
10 International Marketing Strategy	£17.95 ☐	£8.95 ☐	£12.95 ☐
11 Strategic Marketing Management: Planning and Control	£17.95 ☐	£8.95 ☐	£12.95 ☐
12 Strategic Marketing Management: Analysis and Decision (9/00)	£24.95 ☐		

SUBTOTAL £ [ ]

POSTAGE & PACKING

Study Texts

	First	Each extra	
UK	£3.00	£2.00	£ [ ]
Europe*	£5.00	£4.00	£ [ ]
Rest of world	£20.00	£10.00	£ [ ]

Kits/Passcards/Success Tapes

	First	Each extra	
UK	£2.00	£1.00	£ [ ]
Europe*	£2.50	£1.00	£ [ ]
Rest of world	£15.00	£8.00	£ [ ]

Grand Total (Cheques to *BPP Publishing*) I enclose a cheque for (incl. Postage) £ [ ]

Or charge to Access/Visa/Switch

Card Number [ ][ ][ ][ ][ ][ ][ ][ ][ ][ ][ ][ ][ ][ ][ ][ ]

Expiry date [ ]   Start Date [ ]

Issue Number (Switch Only) [ ]

Signature _____

We aim to deliver to all UK addresses inside 5 working days. A signature will be required. Orders to all EU addresses should be delivered within 6 working days.

All other orders to overseas addresses should be delivered within 8 working days.

* Europe includes the Republic of Ireland and the Channel Islands.

REVIEW FORM & FREE PRIZE DRAW

All original review forms from the entire BPP range, completed with genuine comments, will be entered into one of two draws on 31 January 2001 and 31 July 2001. The names on the first four forms picked out on each occasion will be sent a cheque for £50.

Name: _____   Address: _____

_____

_____

How have you used this Kit?
(Tick one box only)

☐ Home study (book only)

☐ On a course: college _____

☐ With 'correspondence' package

☐ Other _____

Why did you decide to purchase this Kit?
(Tick one box only)

☐ Have used complementary Study Text

☐ Have used BPP Kits in the past

☐ Recommendation by friend/colleague

☐ Recommendation by a lecturer at college

☐ Saw advertising

☐ Other _____

During the past six months do you recall seeing/receiving any of the following?
(Tick as many boxes as are relevant)

☐ Our advertisement in *Marketing Success*

☐ Our advertisement in *Marketing Business*

☐ Our brochure with a letter through the post

☐ Our brochure with *Marketing Business*

Which (if any) aspects of our advertising do you find useful?
(Tick as many boxes as are relevant)

☐ Prices and publication dates of new editions

☐ Information on Kit content

☐ Facility to order books off-the-page

☐ None of the above

Have you used the companion Study Text for this subject?   ☐ Yes ☐ No

Your ratings, comments and suggestions would be appreciated on the following areas

	Very useful	Useful	Not useful
Introductory section (Study advice, key questions checklist, etc)	☐	☐	☐
'Do you know' checklists	☐	☐	☐
Tutorial questions	☐	☐	☐
Examination-standard questions	☐	☐	☐
Content of suggested solutions	☐	☐	☐
Quiz	☐	☐	☐
Test paper	☐	☐	☐
Structure and presentation	☐	☐	☐

	Excellent	Good	Adequate	Poor
Overall opinion of this Kit	☐	☐	☐	☐

Do you intend to continue using BPP Study Texts/Kits?   ☐ Yes ☐ No

Please note any further comments and suggestions/errors on the reverse of this page.

Please return to: Kate Machattie, BPP Publishing Ltd, FREEPOST, London, W12 8BR

REVIEW FORM & FREE PRIZE DRAW (continued)

Please note any further comments and suggestions/errors below

FREE PRIZE DRAW RULES

1   Closing date for 31 January 2001 draw is 31 December 2000. Closing date for 31 July 2001 draw is 30 June 2001.

2   Restricted to entries with UK and Eire addresses only. BPP employees, their families and business associates are excluded.

3   No purchase necessary. Entry forms are available upon request from BPP Publishing. No more than one entry per title, per person. Draw restricted to persons aged 16 and over.

4   Winners will be notified by post and receive their cheques not later than 6 weeks after the relevant draw date.

5   The decision of the promoter in all matters is final and binding. No correspondence will be entered into.